Music

Other books in the Careers for the Twenty-First Century series:

Aeronautics
Education
Engineering
Law Enforcement
Medicine
The News Media

Careers
for the
Twenty-First
Century

Music

By Peggy J. Parks

**LUCENT
BOOKS®**

THOMSON

™

GALE

San Diego • Detroit • New York • San Francisco • Cleveland
New Haven, Conn. • Waterville, Maine • London • Munich

Cover: Gwen Stefani and Eve perform at the BET awards.

LIBRARY OF CONGRESS CATALOGING-IN-PUBLICATION DATA

Parks, Peggy J., 1951–
    Music / by Peggy J. Parks.
        p. cm. — (Careers for the 21st century)
Summary: Covers the various positions available in the field of music, discussing
qualifications, training, job opportunities, and technological advances.
Includes bibliographical references (p.   ) and index.
    ISBN 1-59018-223-5 (hardback : alk. paper)
    1. Music—Vocational guidance—Juvenile literature. [1. Music—Vocational guidance.
2. Vocational guidance.] I. Title. II. Careers for the 21st century (San Diego, Calif.)
    ML3928 .P37 2003
    780'.23—dc21

                                                                        2002006019

Printed in the United States of America

Contents

Foreword

Young people in the twenty-first century are faced with a dizzying array of possibilities for careers as they become adults. However, the advances of technology and a world economy in which events in one nation increasingly affect events in other nations have made the job market extremely competitive. Young people entering the job market today must possess a combination of technological knowledge and an understanding of the cultural and socioeconomic factors that affect the working world. Don Tapscott, internationally known author and consultant on the effects of technology in business, government, and society, supports this idea, saying, "Yes, this country needs more technology graduates, as they fuel the digital economy. But . . . we have an equally strong need for those with a broader [humanities] background who can work in tandem with technical specialists, helping create and manage the [workplace] environment." To succeed in this job market young people today must enter it with a certain amount of specialized knowledge, preparation, and practical experience. In addition, they must possess the drive to update their job skills continually to match rapidly occurring technological, economic, and social changes.

Young people entering the twenty-first–century job market must carefully research and plan the education and training they will need to work in their chosen career. High school graduates can no longer go straight into a job where they can hope to advance to positions of higher pay, better working conditions, and increased responsibility without first entering a training program, trade school, or college. For example, aircraft mechanics must attend schools that offer Federal Aviation Administration–accredited programs. These programs offer a broad-based curriculum that requires students to demonstrate an understanding of the basic principles of flight, aircraft function, and electronics. Students must also master computer technology used for diagnosing problems and show that they can apply what they learn toward routine maintenance and any number of needed repairs. With further education, an aircraft mechanic can gain increasingly specialized licenses that place him or her in the job market for positions of higher pay and greater responsibility.

In addition to technology skills, young people must understand how to communicate and work effectively with colleagues or clients from diverse backgrounds. James Billington, librarian of Congress, ascertains that "we do not have a global village, but rather a globe on which there are a whole lot of new villages . . . each trying to get its own place in the world, and anybody who's going to deal with this world is going to have to relate better to more of it." For example, flight attendants are increasingly being expected to know one or more foreign languages in order for them to better serve the needs of international passengers. Electrical engineers collaborating with a sister company in Russia on a project must be aware of cultural differences that could affect communication between the project members and, ultimately, the success of the project.

The Lucent Books Careers for the Twenty-First Century series discusses how these ideas come into play in such competitive career fields as aeronautics, biotechnology, computer technology, engineering, education, law enforcement, and medicine. Each title in the series discusses from five to seven different careers available in the respective field. The series provides a comprehensive view of what it's like to work in a particular job and what it takes to succeed in it. Each chapter encompasses a career's most recent trends in education and training, job responsibilities, the work environment and conditions, special challenges, earnings, and opportunities for advancement. Primary and secondary source quotes enliven the text. Sidebars expand on issues related to each career, including topics such as gender issues in the workplace, personal stories that demonstrate exceptional on-the-job experiences, and the latest technology and its potential for use in a particular career. Every volume includes an Organizations to Contact list as well as annotated bibliographies. Books in this series provide readers with pertinent information for deciding on a career, and a launching point for further research.

Introduction

Music for Life

"Music is everywhere—in bird song and in bubbling brooks and in laughter, even in the stars. Music is the universal language that transcends time and space."[1] Nationally syndicated radio host Paul Harvey once spoke those words, and they ring true for everyone who loves music and believes it is not a luxury, but rather an essential part of life.

Whether their preference is Beethoven or Bach, Miles Davis or Ella Fitzgerald, Elvis Presley or Led Zeppelin, people who have a deep fondness for music could not imagine life without it—nor would they want to. To them, music is practically as important as breathing. Many people learn to play an instrument or sing at a very young age, studying with private music instructors as well as taking music classes in school and college. They often enjoy performing with bands, orchestras, or choral groups, as well as listening to many different kinds of music and attending concerts and musical theater productions. Even the books and magazines music lovers choose to read often relate to music in some way, as do the bulk of their hobbies and activities.

Still, for many people it is one thing to love music and quite another to be serious enough about music to make it their life's work. Their perception may be one of starving musicians or aspiring wanna-be performers who can barely scrape together enough money to pay the bills—although this does not necessarily depict reality. Even if someone is avid about pursuing a music-related career, society does not always support this idea. A high school student who wants to be a music major in college may be discouraged by his or her parents, and advised to focus on a business-related career instead. A talented composer hears only about the competitiveness of the music business, and little about what opportunities might be available. An aspiring music teacher hears nightmare stories about drastic cuts in arts funding and is questioned about the value of music as a part of education. Even the most talented musician is likely to be advised to forget about a career in music and get a so-called real job.

However, in spite of discouragement, negative perceptions, or advice to the contrary, there are many people who pursue music-related careers. And the reason they do this is simple: They feel as though they have music in their blood. Of course, not all those who lean toward music careers become professional performers, nor do they necessarily want to be. They just want music and their careers to be woven together in some way.

People who are interested in music careers have many different choices open to them. Of course, the skills and training they require will vary based on which branch of music they choose to pursue. Those interested in professional music-making might consider becoming composers, performers, or recording engineers, while people interested in the business side of the music industry may choose

An interest in music at a young age can one day lead to a career in music.

to become music publicists. And those interested in careers that involve teaching or counseling may lean toward becoming music educators or music therapists.

No matter what specific area they pursue, people who choose music careers feel so strongly about it that nothing or no one could possibly discourage them from going after their dreams. Music has always been so much a part of their existence that it is perfectly natural for their careers to revolve around it.

Music lover Tom Batiuk is a nationally known cartoonist and creator of the cartoon series *Funky Winkerbean*, and serves on the Advisory Council for the National Association for Music Education. Batiuk shares his thoughts about music, which aptly describe the spirit of people who work in music careers:

> From Chopin to Chuck Berry, . . . the music has always been there. From piano lessons, to marching band, to the sounds coming from a car radio on [a] summer's evening, music has always been with me in my life. Is there anything that can evoke all the nuances of a memory like hearing an old song? It's as if the very emotions are encoded on the notes themselves. And as I listen to the nursery rhymes playing on my son's record player as he falls asleep, it's come the full circle. To imagine a home, a school, or a life without music is to imagine the dreariest of existences. [2]

Chapter 1

Composers

All music, from the past or from the present, was at one time conceived and written by a composer. Whether people hear music on the radio or on a television show, in a movie or performed in a live concert, in a commercial or in a video game, a composer created it. And the music composers create comes in an infinite variety of styles and types from classical to jazz, blues to country, rock to hip hop. Some music is considered to be stand-alone, which means there is no vocal accompaniment, while other music includes lyrics. In the words of composer Curtis S.D. Macdonald, "All types of music can be composed, and composers through hard work and training, can create anything they hear in their head . . . music that can tug at your heart or music that scares you to death."[3]

Famous composers from the eighteenth and nineteenth centuries include Johann Sebastian Bach, Ludwig van Beethoven, Antonio Vivaldi, and Wolfgang Amadeus Mozart, all brilliant musicians who

Composers create music. Many early composers began their music training in childhood.

composed some of the most beloved classical music ever heard. Twentieth-century composer Richard Rodgers is heralded as one of the greatest writers in American musical theater. Two prominent African American composers were Scott Joplin, who was known as the most influential composer of ragtime music, and the legendary Duke Ellington, one of the leading composers of American jazz.

Types of Composers

Just as there is a distinct difference between music composed by Bach and music by Duke Ellington, there are many different types of musical composers. Some, like Rodgers, have specialized in creating music for musical stage productions. His partnership with Oscar Hammerstein resulted in such timeless musical productions as *Oklahoma!*, *Carousel*, *South Pacific*, *The King and I*, and *The Sound of Music*, and the songs from these musicals are as famous as the musicals themselves.

Some composers create music for bands or solo performing artists who perform it live, or record and sell it to millions of fans. Symphony orchestras and opera companies often perform the classical music created by early composers, as well as original pieces created by modern composers. Some composers specialize in creating music for television shows and motion pictures, or music that is played during commercials. And still others create the background music heard in video arcades or computer video games.

Composers often specialize in more than one type of music, and create music for different uses. Macdonald creates many styles, from jazz to blues to dramatic "underscore" (background music), and his compositions are used in movies, television programs, video games, infomercials, and exercise videos. He explains the diversity of his music: "I can capture any style from any period or genre. Music changes and evolves and I like keeping up with the present as well as referring to a grand history of great composers."[4]

There are some composers, like Tommy Tallarico of Orange County, California, who focus their energies and talents on one specialty. Tallarico composes music for video games, and he has created music for popular games such as *Earthworm Jim*, *Disney's Aladdin*, *The Terminator*, *Tomorrow Never Dies*, *Spider-Man*, and *Maximo*, as well as creating the sound design (music and sound effects) for top-selling video games like *Tony Hawk Skateboarding*, *Blitz Football*, and *Unreal 2*. He says he has loved music his whole life and since his sec-

Duke Ellington was a famous American composer of the 1920s and 1930s.

ond love is video games, being able to combine his two loves into a career is a dream come true:

> When I was a kid, I always dreamed of doing something cool and special when I grew up. I think that's true of every kid, actually. But how could I possibly know it would be this cool? I mean, I get up every day, play video games and write music or create sounds for them. It doesn't get any better than that. I'm doing exactly what I want to do, and I consider myself very fortunate.[5]

Creating Music

Composers are highly creative people who compose music in their own individual ways. Thus, there is no clearly defined process for composing music, and no two composers follow the same steps when creating their music. However, all composers—no matter what kind of music they create—use melody and harmony, as well as rhythm patterns and tempo (timing,) to create unique musical pieces.

Some write their music on paper first, while others compose by improvising, or creating the music on their synthesizers or computers. Those who start by writing on paper create scores, which are musical charts that show all the different parts of the music, including the notes for various instruments or instrumental sections.

Macdonald says composing can be compared to building with Legos, where someone builds with all types of shapes and colors. His practice is to start by sketching the music on paper, to get a graphic idea of how it will flow. Then using his computer, he begins to "realize" the piece, bringing it to life as he performs the different parts of the music by using the sounds of various instruments. As he works on creating the music he sometimes follows his written sketch exactly, or he might improvise on the spot, and he keeps working on it until he has achieved exactly what he wants. He calls his creation a musical puzzle, and he continues to fill in the blanks with the right sounds as he composes. For Macdonald, it takes about thirty minutes to compose one minute's worth of music.

Scott Nesbit, a musician and composer from Muskegon, Michigan, uses a more improvisational style. He hears a melody in his head, which inspires him to create the song, then he sits at his synthesizer and builds the piece a little at a time, using various instrumental sounds like guitar, bass, keyboards, violins, cellos, and drums. As he composes, he records the music on tape; if he is happy with it, he will redo the piece later in a music studio. Nesbit says this about his method of composing: "My music stems from my emotions, my imagination. I really envision it as theme music, perhaps for a film. And even though I can read music and write out music notation, I find that to be a slow process, so improvising seems to be the most effective method for me."[6]

Although composers sometimes create music for rock bands and solo artists, many of these performers compose their own music. Chad Kroeger, lead singer and guitarist of the Canadian rock group Nickelback, talks about how he creates the music for his band:

> I come up with the "riff," [which is] the main structure of the song. I come up with the melody, I write the lyrics and then I bring it to the guys and they throw their spice into the spaghetti sauce and what you hear is what you get. . . . I'll hum some things and find the melody that I want and then I'll start spitting out a few sentences here and there and it all starts to come together and then I find the direction of the song. I don't usually write the song, the song kind of writes itself, I guess. 'Cause I'll just sort of be mumbling things and

humming stuff and a couple of words will pop out . . . then I'll have a couple of sentences and then the song just starts to take a direction. . . . It's like, the sculptor. . . . He just starts chipping away and its starts to form itself and then he looks at it and says, "I know what this is!" And he just chips it all away and there it is. [7]

Another composer who uses this free-flowing method is Tallarico, who says that composing music for video games is similar to creating music for movies. His process is to start by playing the video game without sound, until he begins hearing music in his head. Then he runs up three flights of stairs to his studio and starts creating the music on his synthesizer. He admits his process is highly unusual:

> People can always tell when I'm composing because what they hear all day long is me running up and down the stairs about a million times, and I'm not exaggerating either. One thing's for sure, it's a great way to keep fit! I don't know how to read and write music so I just play by ear while I compose—although playing by ear can get rather painful after I've banged my head on the piano all day. [8]

Preparing to Be a Composer

Tallarico began his musical training when he was quite young, starting to learn piano when he was only three years old. Macdonald also started early, learning the drums when he was seven and later teaching himself to improvise piano music for the programs he watched on television. It is common for aspiring composers to take a combination of private music lessons and music classes in middle school and high school, so by the time they reach college age they are proficient in one or more instruments.

A college degree is not always necessary for composers because what counts most is their knowledge and understanding of music, as well as their talent and ability to create it. However, those who do study music in college learn about music history, music theory, and composition, which can help them not only as they compose music but also in communicating with other professionals in the music industry. While in college they can also learn technical subjects such as computer music technology (including synthesizer

Composers and New Technology

Composers create not only the words to music but also musical sounds like pitch, melody, harmony, and tempo (timing). Since their jobs involve creating many different sounds, they often use synthesizers—versatile electronic instruments that can imitate other instruments such as violins, flutes, horns, and drums, as well as create completely new sounds not heard before.

The name *synthesizer* comes from the word *synthesize*, which means putting together parts or elements to form the whole. And that is exactly what synthesizers do: They combine parts and elements of sounds to form a whole sound. The first synthesizers invented in the 1950s were as large as bookshelves and cost hundreds of thousands of dollars. Over the years synthesizers were perfected and became less complicated, as well as smaller and more affordable. Today they are usually equipped with piano-style keyboards, and can be programmed by using switches on the keys as well as digital push buttons, touch-sensitive screens, and computers.

One form of advanced technology known as Musical Instrument Digital Interface (MIDI) improves a synthesizer operator's ability to create and control sound. MIDI technology also works with personal computers, in effect turning them into music-making machines that sound like one instrument or an entire orchestra. In an article on his website entitled "Welcome to a Brave New (Musical) World," composer Donald Griffin says that advanced technology has enhanced his ability to create music, adding:

> I can hear my music the second I create it. I have a nearly infinite variety of musical instruments at my disposal and I can try out new ideas that I can't hear in my head to see if they have merit with very little effort. . . . After hearing a finished tune I can easily make major changes and hear it again with no muss and no fuss. If I had access to these amazing tools when I was just starting out there is no telling what I could have learned or how fast I would have gotten to this point.

techniques), film and video sound effects, and digital editing. In general, the more music-related knowledge, education, and experience aspiring composers have, the more qualified they will be to land their first composing job.

Composer John Williams has created music for more than eighty movies including *Harry Potter and the Sorcerer's Stone*, *Star Wars*, *Jaws*, *Raiders of the Lost Ark*, and *Superman*. He shares the following advice with young people interested in a composing career:

> Reading is enormously important, for inspiration and creation of music. There is more music to be found in poetry and in the quiet contemplation of nature than in studying music itself. . . . As to how to develop a career, one can now have one in music education, or in film, or in a community service, in vocal music, choral, all of these areas. All are rich areas, and are good ones. So a good solid basic education can lead you to a career that is joyful and enormously rewarding.[9]

Traits of a Composer

Whether they compose music for movies, symphonies, or video games, one quality all composers share is an appreciation of music. In fact, most composers remember being immersed in it for most of their lives, as Macdonald explains:

> The jazz that was driven into me when I was young was the most inspirational—Bill Evans, Bob James, and Miles Davis, to name a few. In fact, I was listening to jazz as my peers were into rock and roll. . . . I was inspired and studied many great composers' work such as Beethoven, Mozart, Samuel Barber, Aaron Copland, Bela Bartok, and many more. All of this gave me a well-rounded background to tackle anything that is asked of me today.[10]

Because of the way they feel about music, composers have an almost overpowering desire to create and perform it. This means they are naturally talented and creative people who are not afraid to experiment and try new things as they compose. They have a thirst for knowledge about music and anything music related and they have a desire to keep building their knowledge and perfecting their musical talents. And of course they need an excellent ear for music so they can create the various melodies and harmonies that give their music texture, or richness.

Composers have to constantly interact with people so the ability to relate well to others, both in terms of listening and expressing ideas, is important for them. They must be able to work under tight deadlines, and be open to criticism from those who review and critique their compositions. And since songwriting is a highly competitive field, composers must be able to face rejection and disappointment, since even the most talented composers sometimes wait years before they actually become successful in selling their work. Williams talks about the hard work, self-discipline, and determination that composers need:

Composers are often consulted about their creations. Below, Igor Stravinsky (seated) is asked about one of his compositions.

Success in any of these fields takes a long time; it took a long time for me . . . but the hard work has to be sustained at the most difficult times, and you have to try even harder. This kind of tenacity will get those of us who are not geniuses, but mere mortals, over the finish line. It's a field that demands a lot of diligence and self-discipline and a good work ethic. Of course, whenever you face a blank piece of paper, there is always that feeling, "Can I do a good job this time? Will I be as good as I was last week?" Whatever field we are in we all deal with that. Not everything we do is the highest level that we could achieve.[11]

High Notes and Low Notes

This tenacity and willingness to work hard is something with which composers are very familiar, yet most of them could hardly imagine doing anything else. Their passion for creating music continuously drives them, and their greatest joy is composing music, as Tallarico explains: "I'm having loads of fun doing my job. Yes, there are tons of challenges and hard work, and lots of traveling around, and that can be tough sometimes. But I love doing what I do and have been at it for over ten years now. When it stops being fun is when I'll stop doing it. But I really don't see that happening, at least not anytime soon."[12] Most composers would agree that creating music is extremely satisfying and fulfilling, especially when they sell something they have created and hear their music being played—which is the culmination of all their hard work and effort.

Like any career, being a composer has its downside. It can take a long time, possibly years, to sell a musical score or even to get someone to pay attention to a new composer's work. Since many composers work as freelancers, meaning they work for themselves as well as by themselves, they often work alone and can feel isolated from other music professionals. And the old saying "feast or famine" definitely applies to people who compose for a living—months can pass by without any work and then suddenly a project may come along that has to be created in a seemingly impossible time frame.

Opportunities

Perhaps the biggest challenge aspiring composers must face is competition. Composing is a highly competitive field and people with the most talent and commitment are the most likely to succeed.

A Composer Who Could Not Hear

In the music world, there is perhaps no one more famous than Ludwig van Beethoven. Born in 1770, Beethoven was the son of a town musician who expected him to follow in the steps of Mozart, a child prodigy who was composing symphonies at the age of eight. Although Beethoven did not exhibit signs of musical brilliance at such an early age as Mozart, he did publish his first set of piano variations at the age of thirteen. Throughout his early adult years, he was hailed as a musical genius and a master of piano improvisation, and by the time he was in his early twenties, he had composed many popular musical works.

When Beethoven was in his late twenties, tragedy struck: He began to experience lapses in his hearing. Filled with despair over the affliction he felt certain would end his ability to create music as well as end his life, he wrote this to his brothers in a will-like document called the "Heiligenstädter Testament," included in its entirety in the *Classical Music Pages Quarterly:* "But what a humiliation for me when someone standing next to me heard a flute in the distance and I heard nothing, or someone standing next to me heard a shepherd sing and again I heard nothing."

However, Beethoven's life did not end because of his deafness, nor did he lose his ability to compose. He once said he had always heard the various instrumental parts in his head before actually listening to them—now that skill enabled him to continue composing in his mind. Beethoven lived for twenty-five years after writing about his hearing loss, and in spite of his growing deafness, and losing his ability to perform as a pianist, he created some of his most brilliant and acclaimed works. Even after he was completely deaf he continued to compose, creating his famous Symphony No. 9 in D Minor with no ability to hear his music. As he made plans to compose a tenth symphony Beethoven caught a serious cold, which led to a complicated illness. He died at the age of fifty-six. Over two centuries later, his musical legacy lives on.

Because so many composers work as freelancers, there are no accurate figures to show exactly how many composers there are, or how many there will be tomorrow. Yet even though it is a competitive field, opportunities exist for those with enough talent and determination to make it in the music business. In fact, as long as there are movies, television shows, concerts, video games—for that matter, any form of music at all—there will be a need for composers to create the music.

Macdonald urges aspiring composers not to give up on their dreams, and he offers the following advice about perseverance: "If anyone can do it, you can too. Finding work is up to you. Get in touch with directors and producers of projects. They are the decision makers and they are the people who will listen to your music and decide if they want to hire you. . . . The more experience you have, the more likely you'll be to get the work."[13]

Variable Earnings

Composers like Macdonald, Williams, Tallarico, and others like them have worked for many years to get where they are, and the salaries they make usually reflect the success and recognition they have achieved. However, the reality is that many aspiring composers have a difficult time making enough money to live on. Because of this, most have steady jobs in other fields and compose music on the side as they wait for their first break into the music business. People who compose music for a living say that building a career as a composer is a bit like climbing a ladder—once they sell the first composition, they have reached the first rung. The more music they sell, the more credibility they earn in the industry, and the higher they will be able to climb.

According to a national report on salaries for music-related careers, composers earn average salaries of between $28,000 and $83,000 per year, and those with a college education typically earn the most. The National Association for Music Education reports an extremely wide variance in salaries: A composer of music for television shows can earn from $1,000 to $5,000 or higher per thirty-minute episode, and a composer of film scores can earn from $2,000 to $200,000 or higher per film. Of course, the salaries composers earn vary considerably based on experience, level of expertise, the type of music they compose, and geographic location.

Famous Women Composers

Two of the most famous names in musical composition are Schumann and Mendelssohn, and the fame associated with these names is most often attributed to Robert Schumann and Felix Mendelssohn. However, many people are not aware that Schumann's wife, Clara, and Mendelssohn's sister, Fanny, were brilliant composers in their own right.

In the nineteenth century when these two women were creating music, composing was not considered acceptable for women. If they were fortunate enough to be trained in music at all, it was usually because they were born into a musical family, as were both Schumann and Mendelssohn. Playing music was acceptable—but composing was not. Mendelssohn's father once wrote to her that Felix would likely make music his profession, but she should view music as "an ornament," and should never expect anything beyond that. Yet although her efforts were frowned upon, Mendelssohn continued to compose music, even though most of her compositions were never published.

Clara Schumann's story was different from Mendelssohn's because both her father and her famous husband encouraged her to compose. In an essay entitled "Review of Clara's Music," reprinted on British composer and pianist Diane Ambache's website, Robert Schumann wrote about the music his wife created:

> Let Bach penetrate to a depth where even the miner's lamp is threatened with extinction; let Beethoven lash out at the clouds with his titan's fists; whatever our own time has produced in terms of heights and depths—she grasps it all, and recounts it with a charming, maidenly wisdom . . . she has raised her own standards to a degree that leaves one wondering anxiously where it all may lead.

In spite of the encouragement she received, however, Clara Schumann was subject to the prejudices of the times. An 1839 entry in her diary, reprinted on Ambache's website, read: "I once thought that I possessed creative talent, but I have given up this idea; a woman must not desire to compose—not one has been able to do it, and why should I expect to? It would be arrogance, though indeed, my father led me into it in earlier days." Fortunately, unlike Fanny Mendelssohn most of Clara Schumann's music was published.

While all composers may dream of someday reaching the pinnacle of their careers and achieving fame and fortune, that is not what drives most composers. Rather, it is a passion for music and the desire to spend their lives creating it. Williams sums up his feelings about his work and the success he has achieved:

> I couldn't possibly have imagined 20, 30 years ago that I would have had the opportunities that I've had to work with the people I've worked with, the orchestras I've been able to conduct. For me it's a constant challenge every day and . . . a challenge to renew it every day. I work six days a week at writing or performing, and my objective is just to improve and get better if I can. And that's my job. And I've been rewarded beyond my dreams in it. [14]

Chapter 2

Musicians

The stadium is packed and the intro music has begun, filling the air with the sounds of screaming guitars and pounding drums. The fans are going wild, yelling and cheering as they anxiously await the start of the concert. Spotlights pan the ceiling and move across the faces in the audience, and then come to rest on the stage. The band walks out and thousands of people are instantly on their feet, their applause deafening as they show their adoration for the performers. The band picks up their instruments and start to play their latest song, which has recently gone platinum on the charts.

Most every musician has this dream—the dream of becoming a famous star, adored by fans everywhere. Some manage to climb the ladder of success and achieve fame and fortune; most do not. Yet even musicians who never come close to achieving star-studded success still get a great deal of joy out of performing their music, even if it is only in front of a hundred fans instead of twenty thousand.

Dave Matthews is one musician whose group has definitely reached the top. Yet he still seems surprised at the popularity his band has achieved since he formed it in 1991. He has this to say about his stardom: "I dreamt about it, and stumbled with it and found myself here—with a lot of work in between. At 19 I was sitting behind a computer at a little store selling software, and I think I was dreaming about getting up and playing music but I didn't know if it was going to happen. I'm no more of a musician than I was five years ago, it's just that more people know I'm a musician."[15]

From Guitarists to Opera Singers

The term *musician* describes not only pop artists like Matthews but also a diverse variety of other musical artists. A bass guitarist in a country western band is as much a musician as a pianist who performs Mozart concertos with the San Francisco Symphony. Folk singers and opera singers are musicians, as are members of so-called boy bands like the Backstreet Boys and *NSYNC. There are musicians who play guitar for television commercials and those who perform in musical acts at resorts, those who sing in Broadway theater productions and those who play the drums for jazz bands. Basically, anyone who plays musical instruments or sings, either solo or as part of a group, is a musician. And some achieve enough success in their careers to make a living doing what they love to do the most: performing music.

Musicians, whether they play instruments or sing, usually specialize in a particular kind of music or performance style. Instrumental musicians may perform in a large band or orchestra, or with a small four- or five-member combo. Some play more than one instrument, such as both guitar and keyboards, which makes them more versatile

Dave Matthews, who started as a local musician in Charlottesville, Virginia, is now a multi-platinum artist and performs in large stadiums such as Giants Stadium in New Jersey.

and therefore more valuable to other group members. Singers, who may perform as backup vocalists for a group or as featured soloists, usually have their own styles and the type of music they sing often depends on their vocal range (soprano, contralto, tenor, or baritone), as well as the type of music they most enjoy. Some prefer opera, some prefer reggae, and still others prefer to sing country western, rock, or folk.

Wherever There Is Music

Just as there are all kinds of musicians, there are all kinds of places where musicians perform. Instrumentalists who play with symphony orchestras, opera companies, or musical theater groups usually perform in theaters or auditoriums located in the cities where they live. Some instrumentalists perform with small chamber music groups like trios or quartets, and they may play anywhere from large auditoriums or theaters to small venues (locations) such as churches or schools, where they make guest appearances.

The New York Philharmonic (below) plays classical music for large audiences in symphony halls.

The Grammy Awards

Considered the recording industry's most prestigious award, the Grammy is presented annually by an organization called the Recording Academy. Founded in 1957 by a group of Los Angeles music professionals and record-label executives, the Academy sought a way to recognize and celebrate the artistic achievement of talented musicians and singers, as well as behind-the-scenes contributors such as producers and engineers. Thus, the Grammy Award was born.

Grammys are intended to honor excellence in the recording arts and sciences, and the annual Grammy Awards presentation brings together thousands of creative and technical recording industry professionals from all over the world. Each year, Grammys are awarded for twenty-eight separate musical categories including pop, gospel, classical, and others, and there are 101 categories within those fields. Also, other awards are given at the Grammy presentation, which fall outside the framework of the Grammy category; these recognize contributions and activities of significance to the recording field such as the Lifetime Achievement Award, the Trustees Award, the Grammy Hall of Fame Award, the Technical Grammy Award, and the Grammy Legend Award.

The Grammy Awards presentation is one of the most widely watched shows on television. Each year the Grammy ceremonies are telecast to an international audience of over 2 billion people in 180 countries.

Many musicians perform in nightclubs and restaurants on a regular basis, and some also hire themselves out to play at small, private events like wedding receptions and parties. Well-known musicians often perform at large festivals, parades, and other special events that are held either indoors in auditoriums or halls, or outdoors in large parks or open-air arenas. Some musicians perform in shows at popular vacation destinations like Walt Disney World's Epcot Center and Six Flags, and others perform on cruise ships or at casinos and nightclubs in Las Vegas and other cities. Some musicians spend much of their time touring, and playing in relatively large venues around the country.

In addition to performing live, musicians who record music spend time working at studios where they have access to soundproof rooms and high-tech equipment like amplifiers, headphones, microphones, sound-mixing equipment, and recording equipment. Also, there are musicians known as session musicians who work at recording studios and play backup music for other singers and groups.

More Than Just Performing

Wherever musicians happen to work, it is usually obvious that they love doing what they do and have fun doing it. However, a musician's career is about more than just performing—it also involves a tremendous amount of work. Unless musicians are content to perform music written by other people, they put a lot of time into writing their own music and then spend many hours rehearsing it. If they record a CD, they may spend days or even weeks in recording sessions. Those who are starting out or are relatively unknown must book their own gigs and try to get media attention by setting up interviews at radio stations, talking with newspaper entertainment editors, or arranging CD promotions at music stores. And of course, there is the business side of professional performing, which involves keeping track of money earned and paying expenses.

Another important (and often grueling) task is setup and teardown at gigs. With the exception of big-name performers who have road crews to take care of this work, musicians must handle it themselves, and it can involve hours of work. Jeff Abercrombie, bass guitarist for the rock band Fuel, talks about what this was like for his band: "Our life consisted of driving to the gig, setting it up, playing our show, breaking down the P.A. [public-address system], driving back home. Then doing it all again the next day and just on and on. We persevered."[16]

Carl Bell, Fuel's guitarist, adds his perspective on the amount of work involved with being a professional musician: "Nothing in this business is easy. Nothing. We've been working really, really hard for a long time and are totally dedicated to making it happen."[17]

What It Takes to Make It

Even though becoming a professional musician requires a lot of hard work, the most important quality every musician needs is talent. Some talent, like a beautiful singing voice or the ability to easily play instruments, may come naturally, but it takes years of practice and training to develop talent to a professional level. And doing that requires commitment and motivation on the part of the musician, as well as a healthy dose of self-discipline.

Jacey Bedford is part of the vocal trio Artisan, a folk group from England that performs throughout Europe, the United States, and Canada. She talks about what it takes to make it as a professional musician: "You can decide to go pro and make a career plan but unless you've got two essential ingredients, talent and determination, you won't make it work. . . . Twelve and a half years later we're still sane and still enjoying it."[18]

Musicians not only need to be determined but also to believe in themselves and their abilities. Even if they are not confident by nature, those who aspire to perform professionally must develop self-confidence. When they have opportunities to perform live, it is common for them to suffer from stage fright (especially at first), but this is something all musicians must eventually learn to overcome. And part of this is learning to handle rejection—having the willingness and the courage to keep trying, even when it would be much

Why Are They Still Called Records?

In this age of high technology and sophisticated digital recording, the only vinyl records that are still around are left over from another era. No one actually makes *records* anymore and musicians do not record *albums* anymore. Yet those terms are still used. Listening to a radio station, one hears: "This might just be the best record this band has ever made" or "This album is headed for the top of the charts." There are record stores and record labels and record company executives and record promotion, as well as record producers, record distributors, record sales, and record contracts. Even though vinyl records have been replaced by compact discs (CDs), the word *record* is still commonly used. Sometimes people use it as an abbreviation for *recording*. And sometimes it is just difficult to let go of words that bring back memories of the good old days of rock and roll.

easier to give up. Booking agent and music publicity expert Ariel Hyatt says: "Trying to make a living making music is not for the meek. If you are not willing to work very hard and have a lot of doors slammed in your face, don't try to make a go of this . . . if you can . . . plow forward taking risks and not taking no for an answer, things will begin to happen."[19]

However, even when musicians have all the confidence and determination in the world, they cannot make it professionally without being committed to practicing and rehearsing on a regular basis. Mindy Kaufman, a professional flutist who performs with the New York Philharmonic, says this about regular practice:

> Like Horowitz [famous Russian pianist] used to say, "If I miss one day, I know it; if I miss two days, my wife knows it; and if I miss three days, everybody knows it." I will practice anywhere from one to three hours a day. . . . It's almost like play-

Members of Jefferson Starship, a band popular in the 70s and 80s, spend time in a recording studio. Musicians often go into the studio to rehearse and analyze their performances.

ing tennis, where you have to work on your serve, your backhand, your forehand, the lob—you have all these different shots, and you have to work on all of them because they're all part of the game. [20]

Education and Training

Musicians like Kaufman, who perform with symphony orchestras or opera companies, almost always have college degrees as well as extensive training in classical music. However, just as styles of music vary from musician to musician, the amount of education and training varies as well. Some have years of formal training with private instructors or in music programs in colleges and music schools. Others have little or no formal training, and have developed their natural talent and skills through years of self-teaching and diligent practice.

Young people interested in becoming musicians would benefit from studying music, and by becoming involved in as many music-related activities as possible. Performing in a school band, orchestra, or choir; being part of a church musical group; or playing in a band with friends can provide excellent experience, as does participating in school and community musical theater productions.

The Life of a Musician

Many young people who dream about becoming professional musicians are enticed by the magic of performing onstage. And performing is definitely what musicians find most exhilarating, as Bedford of Artisan explains: "You can't really beat the feeling of walking out onto a stage and having twelve hundred people leap to their feet cheering. Okay, that doesn't happen every time but when it does, it makes up for all those times you've played to three people and the theatre cat." [21] Even lesser-known musicians who perform in smaller venues and clubs enjoy the "rush" of performing before live audiences, as well as having fans buy the original music they write and record.

Musicians who have been fortunate enough to achieve celebrity status enjoy many perks such as first-class treatment wherever they go, the adulation of their fans, packed concerts, and even

Eddie Vedder (second from left), of the band Pearl Jam, has often faced the issue of his privacy being violated. This may make the musician reluctant to deal with the press.

television and movie appearances. Plus, these musicians usually make huge amounts of money, both from their concerts and from record sales.

However, even life as a musical celebrity is not always pleasant. The privacy most people take for granted is often nonexistent for famous musicians, because fans clamor to know everything possible about their favorite stars' lives, and paparazzi, the media people who photograph famous celebrities, hound them almost everywhere they go. Pearl Jam lead singer Eddie Vedder explains how this affects him: "Being a musician feels natural. I always knew I wanted to do it. The hard part was the rock-star thing. I didn't understand it, I didn't understand the attention. It's like . . . there's nothing you can do with it. You lose your privacy. You lose your ability to observe situations without changing them simply by entering." [22]

Another downside to being a musical celebrity is that fans can be fickle, so fame can disappear quickly. One year a musician is selling millions of records and is booked solid for a concert tour, then the next year fans may lose interest, sales will drop, and the musician may no longer be in demand. Bedford says the secret is to have the right attitude about performing: "A tiny proportion of people working in the music business are famous, but it can be a here today, gone tomorrow thing. The ones who have a long career are those whose ambition is to be good—not to be famous."[23]

Musicians who manage to become famous often spend much of their time touring; and contrary to popular opinion, this is not necessarily glamorous. In fact, musicians typically find life on the road very stressful. They can get burned out by constant travel and spending months far away from their families and friends. They hop from city to city and from hotel to hotel, and this can become tedious and frustrating. John McCrea, lead singer for the rock group Cake, talks about the harsh realities of touring:

> If anyone thinks it's easy to do, let them leave their homes and families and everything else they know for two years and then come back to discuss it with me. [Touring] is incredibly unrewarding. For a while it's great to go out and play in front of people who clearly want to hear you. But then you realize it's the exact same thing night after night, and you feel less like an "artist" and more like one of those performing bears at Chuck E. Cheese.[24]

Another challenge all professional musicians must deal with—whether they are famous or not—is the challenge of unpredictable schedules. Kaufman works five or six days a week with the orchestra, and even though performing with the New York Philharmonic is radically different from being a musician in a nightclub, the work schedule is not all that different. She rehearses with the orchestra about twenty hours a week and performs in concerts three or four nights a week. She shares her views on the schedule challenges musicians face: "We work on Saturday nights and almost every holiday—if you don't want to work on holidays, if you want to go away on the weekends, you shouldn't be a musician."[25]

Earning Pennies or Earning Millions

Just as musicians must tolerate unpredictability in their schedules, they also must cope with incomes that can fluctuate radically.

Professional drummer Russ Miller, who has worked with hundreds of musical stars, says this is something musicians learn to deal with: "If you're going from gig to gig, you know, one month you make ten times more money than you need and the next month you make half of what you need. It's important to understand how to budget."[26]

Musicians' earnings depend on factors such as how well known and popular they are, where they perform, and how often they perform. Musicians performing in small, local nightclubs are often part-time musicians who have other steady jobs, and they can earn as little as a few hundred dollars per performance. Well-known musicians onstage in large clubs, casinos, and resorts may earn thousands of dollars per performance. In New York, orchestra members who work on Broadway earn approximately $63,000 per year, although their earnings vary based on how many shows they are in. Members of large orchestras like the New York Philharmonic typically earn over $90,000 per year. And the most famous musical stars often earn millions of dollars per year, from a combination of concert appearances and royalties from record sales.

What the Future Holds

All musicians—whether they perform with a prominent New York orchestra or an obscure nightclub in Woonsocket, Rhode Island—are aware that the career they have chosen is more risky and uncertain than other careers. In other words, it is easier to find a job and make a living as a computer programmer than as a musician. But since there are approximately a quarter of a million professional musicians working in the United States, opportunities do exist. The *Princeton Review* offers this optimistic perspective: "Music has been around since the beginning of time. Since there can be no music without musicians, their place is virtually assured—even if lucrative recording deals and a place in the limelight will continue to elude many of even the most gifted artists."[27]

The reality is that most musicians, whether full-time or part-time, in small venues or large, will probably never become famous or rich. Yet they would not think of quitting because they love music and performing. With enough talent, motivation, and persistence, musicians can achieve some level of success in their chosen profession. Miller offers these words of encouragement: "I'd hate for a

The Battle Over "Free" Music

It used to be that if someone wanted a song or a collection of songs, they had to purchase it. Then a young man named Shawn Fanning invented a website called Napster, and suddenly everything changed. Music—all kinds of music—was available in a digital format known as MP3, and it was available to anyone with a computer and Internet connection. Fans were delighted. Many people in the recording industry, including some famous musical groups like Metallica, were appalled. Opponents say that it is a rip-off, an insidious virus that will erode the recording industry's ability to market and sell music, and that hurts the artists because it will cheat them out of royalties. In fact, Metallica tried to force this free music sharing to stop. Not all musicians agreed with Metallica, however. Artists like Courtney Love, Limp Bizkit, David Bowie, and the Beastie Boys were supportive of Napster, and believed it could actually help sell CDs by giving music fans a preview of the music before they bought it.

The real issue with online digital music sharing is over copyright infringement, which means ownership: Who actually owns the music? The record labels who produce it? The artists who record it? And should music be as accessible as other information housed among the millions of websites? After being cited for copyright infringement, Napster was officially shut down in July 2001, but many other similar sites have sprung up to take its place. Plus, as of spring 2002, Napster had ironed out most of its legal wrinkles and was ready to launch its new site.

Napster founder Shawn Fanning.

The battle over free music is a complicated legal issue where the question of right versus wrong seems to be more an object of subjective opinion, rather than one of clear-cut legalities. One thing is for certain, however; this is an issue that will undoubtedly be argued, challenged, and unresolved in courtrooms for many years to come.

nineteen-year-old guy to look at me and think, 'Oh, I'll never be able to make a living because I can't play like that.' Yeah, you're right, you can't—yet. I've done thousands of gigs between [age] nineteen and thirty-one, and every one of those experiences makes you a better musician. By the time you're thirty-one, you'll play as well, if not better."[28]

Chapter 3

Music Educators

Music educators are so passionate about music that they have made a career out of sharing that passion, and their knowledge of music, with others. They teach people to sing or to play musical instruments. They teach classes in music history or music appreciation. They lead kindergarteners in choral programs and college marching bands on a football field. Music educators merge their talents and love of music with their desire to help broaden the knowledge of their students. And in doing so, they enrich their students' lives by teaching them about the value, and beauty, of having music in their lives.

These symphony orchestra musicians learned how to play their instruments from music educators.

One music educator shares her feelings about teaching:

> We teach music . . . not because we expect you to major in
> music. Not because we expect you to play or sing all your life.
> . . . But so you will be human. So you will recognize beauty.
> So you will be closer to an infinite beyond this world. So you
> will have something to cling to. So you will have more love,
> more compassion, more gentleness, more good—in short,
> more Life.[29]

Types of Music Educators

People choosing a career in music education have many different
avenues open to them. Some become teachers in elementary schools,
while others teach in secondary (middle or high) schools. Some teach
at the college level, and others become music librarians. And there are
also many people who teach private music lessons, either working on
their own or through an affiliation with a music store or studio.

Elementary music teachers work with students from kindergarten
through fifth or sixth grade. Based on the schools where they teach,
they may have their own classrooms or travel from room to room and
teach in multiple classrooms. Some even cover more than one
school, traveling to different schools on different days of the week.
These teachers often specialize in general music, which includes basic
skills and concepts such as reading music notes, counting, and scales.
They teach younger children how to move together rhythmically as
a group, as well as how to sing and harmonize. And some elementary
music teachers specialize in instrument instruction, teaching children
how to play band or orchestral instruments like the French horn,
flute, clarinet, or drums; however, these classes are usually reserved for
upper elementary grades.

In secondary schools, music teachers may teach band, orchestra,
or choir. They also teach other classes such as music theory, which
involves learning how to read and write music, as well as studying
melody, harmony, rhythm, and musical terminology; music appreciation, which is the study of famous classical composers and their
music; and music history, which involves studying the history of a
variety of different musical styles.

Most colleges and universities have music departments and
some, like New York's Juilliard School or Boston's Berklee College

The World-Famous Juilliard School

In terms of musical excellence, there is no more esteemed honor than having the name Juilliard School attached to one's résumé. Founded in 1905, the Juilliard School was originally known as the Institute of Musical Art, and was established to rival the famed musical conservatories in Europe; prior to that, most U.S. students pursued their musical studies in Europe.

When wealthy textile merchant Augustus D. Juilliard died in 1919, his will contained the largest single bequest for the advancement of music. Several new divisions were formed, and in 1926 the school became known as the Juilliard School of Music. Today the prestigious school has three divisions—music, dance, and drama—and is located in the heart of New York City. The Juilliard School houses over two hundred pianos; thirty-five private teaching studios; scenery and costume shops where materials are produced for opera, dance, and drama presentations; and fifteen two-story studios where rehearsals and workshops are held. There are also two theaters: the Juilliard Theater, which seats nearly one thousand people, and the Drama Theater, which seats two hundred. The Juilliard School's Alice Tully Hall is its most famous auditorium and the site of concerts by students and professionals. It is known for extraordinary acoustics and its 4,192-pipe organ; and it is home to the Juilliard Orchestra, the Juilliard Symphony, and the Chamber Music Society of Lincoln Center.

Because the Juilliard School is considered the créme de la créme of music schools, many of its faculty members are accomplished musicians, as well as music educators. Juilliard professors have performed with major orchestras and operas all over the world as soloists, orchestra members, chamber musicians, and conductors. Those teaching composition and music theory are successful composers who have created music for major symphonies and operas, and have been the recipients of a variety of international awards, including the Pulitzer Prize. Many faculty members at Juilliard have previously worked as music educators at prestigious conservatories and universities.

It has been written that Juilliard's graduate list reads like a who's who of the performing arts world. The same could be said about the school's impressive group of educators.

of Music, specialize in music education. The music professors who teach in higher-education institutions are usually expected to specialize in one or two areas like music theory or music history, and some teach musical composition, musical arranging, or instrumental or vocal performance. Other professors specialize in music education—teaching students how to become music teachers.

Private music instructors teach private or group lessons in vocal and instrumental music. In many cases these professionals are self-employed and teach out of their homes, or travel to the homes of their students. Or they may have business relationships with music schools, studios, or music stores, so they are likely to teach lessons wherever these establishments are located. Private instructors often teach music only part-time, while being employed at other jobs. For example, many music teachers and professional musicians, as well as those who are employed in nonmusic careers, also teach private music lessons on the side.

Another kind of music educator is the music librarian, a professional who is extensively trained in music. Most music librarians work for large research libraries such as the Library of Congress or the New York Public Library, or in the music section of university or college libraries. Other organizations that employ music librarians include radio or television stations, musical societies or foundations, and performing groups like symphony orchestras or opera companies.

Sharing Knowledge with Others

Specific responsibilities for music educators vary based on where they work, and the age group of their students. However, the one common thread that ties them all together is that their careers are devoted to helping others learn about music.

No matter what subject they teach—general music, music theory, music history, instrumental music, choir, or a combination of music-related classes—music educators must have a deep understanding of the subject matter. They prepare a detailed class outline called a syllabus, so that their students know exactly what is expected of them and understand their goals. Music educators also regularly test their students, to help ensure they are achieving specific class objectives and making progress.

In addition to teaching, music educators keep regular office hours so students may seek their help outside of class. This may involve

Music educators often instruct students on how to perform for different kinds of audiences. The marching band above plays for spectators of a football game during halftime.

helping students with problems they are having in the class, or providing extra instrumental instruction for those who are falling behind.

Another common activity for music educators who teach at the elementary, secondary, or college level is working with student performing groups. Music teachers and professors often act as coaches for pep bands, marching bands, and jazz bands. They may organize and lead special music performances, such as those held during holidays and at the end of the school year. And they may act as music directors and conductors during school musical theater productions.

While music librarians have some responsibilities that are similar to other music educators, the biggest difference is that they usually do not teach in classrooms. They provide library visitors with instructions on how to use the facility and assist with music research. They are responsible for selecting different materials to be housed within the library such as musical scores, books, periodicals, recordings, and sometimes manuscripts and other rare materials. And while all music librarians have similar duties, specific job tasks vary based on where they are employed. Those who work for large public libraries may also help to plan special exhibits and concerts, and teach classes in music theory or music history. They may also work

Metronomes Keep the Beat

When teaching their students how to play musical instruments or to sing, music educators often use a device known as a metronome. Metronomes generate a clicking sound to indicate beats, and they are used to help regulate rhythm when someone is playing an instrument or singing. The metronome was invented in 1812 by Dietrich Nikolaus Winkler of Amsterdam, but it was later copied, enhanced, and patented as a metronome by Johan Maelzel, an inventor of mechanical musical instruments and a friend of Beethoven's. Although a subsequent lawsuit acknowledged Winkler as the instrument's creator, by that time Maelzel had sold many metronomes and was often credited with inventing it.

The first metronomes were pyramid-shaped objects made of wood, and they worked like old-fashioned windup clocks. A pendulum was powered by a windup spring, and a movable weight on the end of the pendulum determined the speed of the beat (tempo). Each time the pendulum swung all the way to one side it caused a loud, mechanical click.

Although pendulum-style metronomes are still available today, the electronic varieties are generally preferred by musicians and teachers. These metronomes are battery powered and have no pendulums or other moving parts. The tempo is set either by turning a dial or by entering digitally the desired number of beats per minute, and the sound generated is a short, electronic ping, a click, a beep, or a flashing light. There are even talking metronomes that identify beats by computerized "spoken" numbers.

A metronome helps musicians keep time by clicking during practice.

Metronomes come in a variety of shapes and styles. Some are as small as a credit card or wristwatch, some are the size of a paperback book, and some are shaped like portable compact disc players. No one style is superior to another, and people usually choose metronomes based on their own personal preferences.

with other community organizations to plan lectures or music-related public programs. Music librarians who work for university or college libraries may be responsible for ordering or renting the music needed by student orchestras, bands, or choir groups. And those employed by professional performing groups like symphony orchestras or opera companies organize and maintain libraries of performance materials for use by their particular group.

Qualities Music Educators Need

Whether someone decides to become a music librarian or to teach music at an elementary school, people who are interested in this profession have several characteristics in common. First, of course, is their love for music and an appreciation for many different styles and types. They must possess musical talent, either in singing or playing one or more instruments, as well as being proficient at reading music. They must also have an insatiable desire to learn everything possible about music—and this motivation to learn does not stop once they become established in their careers. Even those who have worked as music educators for many years continue developing their talents and building their knowledge by taking college classes, participating in seminars or workshops, and reading.

An essential quality for any music educator is the unselfish desire—and the skill—to help others learn. This means they need both patience and sensitivity, as well as a dedication to help students develop their individual talents and abilities. Those who teach in elementary or middle schools need patience, since young children are easily distracted and can be unruly in a classroom setting. Teachers must be able to keep them excited and motivated about music, while still keeping order in the classroom. Plus, these teachers may also need to help students overcome their fears about music; for example, students who do not think they sing well can be encouraged to keep singing and explore their hidden talents. And students who fear they could not play an instrument can be encouraged to keep practicing so they can build their skills.

Music educators need leadership qualities, which enables them to direct their students, and creativity which inspires those whom they teach. They must have the ability to interact with people, including their students as well as other professionals with whom they work and interact. And they must be excellent communicators in both speaking and listening.

The Rewards of Being a Music Educator

Whether music educators teach grade schoolers or high schoolers, whether they work in classrooms or libraries, the most satisfying and fulfilling part of their jobs is the ability to make a positive difference in their students' lives. This can be especially true for music educators who work with students from underprivileged backgrounds. For these young people, music can provide a creative escape—even if their young lives are unsettled or their world seems to be coming apart at the seams, music can help heal and change them. Nancy Barcus, a music teacher in a Waco, Texas, inner-city elementary school, shares this story about the positive difference music has made in the life of one of her students:

> There is Charla, who has lived in a series of houses with her mother—often with no heat, light, or running water—and sometimes practices her violin at a large vacant lot. There several adults sit on abandoned furniture, building a small bonfire to warm themselves, and remain together long hours into the night as children roam and play around the edges of the lot. Charla's violin always comes safely back to school with her, and she hands it in with a smile. . . . As I recall [her] and so many other students, I notice the zest with which children who have less than their share of this world's tangible benefits arrive at school each morning, once they have found something that works for them. I am struck by how much school seems to mean to them.[30]

Another benefit of being a music educator is being able to encourage students to believe that they can learn and succeed in music—and then watching them do just that. After all, young people may be born with a certain amount of natural talent, but it is the music educator who teaches and inspires them, helping them to achieve their goals. Even young students who have no musical knowledge whatsoever can evolve into gifted and talented musicians under the guidance of dedicated music educators.

Maryland professional cellist and music educator Robert Battey says he cannot imagine a life that does not include teaching music, and he talks about the rewards of watching his students develop their musical talents:

When I've been fortunate enough to work with a gifted or highly intelligent student, those lessons have been among the most stimulating experiences of my life. But the more ordinary talents are learning opportunities for me as well. A gifted student can play well standing on her head; the proof of one's ideas is [more evident in] the average students. It is through them, their struggles, and their occasional skepticism that a teaching idea or a technical principle must stand the test of time . . . each student is like a new piece of music; one must unlock their secrets slowly and carefully, applying sound general principles, but seeking out what is different and special in each one.[31]

Challenges Music Educators Face

Playing an important role in developing a child's musical talent is only one of the rewards of a career in music education. However, there are also challenges music educators face. It takes a great deal of patience and perseverance to teach music. This is especially true in large classrooms of young, fidgety children, or when working with

A music educator must know how to keep students motivated and excited about music.

students who are not motivated, or who lack natural musical talent. Educators teaching band or orchestra may have to deal with students who do not practice playing their instruments, and therefore end up playing poorly and trailing their classmates in progress.

Another challenge faced by music educators, particularly those teaching at poorer inner-city elementary schools, is the fear of losing their jobs because of budget cuts in arts education or other reductions in funding. Because schools throughout the United States are funded with tax dollars, there is an ongoing debate about whether the arts, which includes both art- and music-related subjects, should be included as part of the regular curriculum. Some people view subjects like math and science as crucial, while considering music as "icing on the cake"—or something that is nice, but not necessary. And even though many people disagree with this type of thinking, music-teaching jobs are not as plentiful as core curriculum teaching jobs.

For private instructors, the biggest challenge is that they often do not earn enough money to make a living solely by teaching. This means they must work at other jobs as well, which can amount to long hours and weekend work.

A Music Educator's Career Path

Despite the challenges, many people aspire to be music educators because of their feelings about music. And these people often make that choice well before they reach college. By the time they are finished with high school they have developed skills in singing or one or more instruments, and are proficient at reading music. Some activities that help prepare students for music education careers include working at band camps or summer music programs, volunteering to tutor students, or observing music teachers.

College is an absolute requirement for aspiring music educators. Students who are interested in working at elementary or secondary schools need at least a bachelor's degree in music, along with a teaching certificate. An advanced degree, such as a master's degree, is not necessarily required for those teaching music at elementary or secondary schools, but those with advanced degrees are often given first consideration for jobs.

Teaching jobs at colleges and universities require a master's degree, and many schools prefer, or even require, doctoral (Ph.D.) degrees. Aspiring music librarians must earn a minimum of a bach-

Does Music Make Children Smarter?

Music has always been known as something that is good for people's spirits. In his series of papers entitled "Over the Teacups," which appeared in the magazine *Atlantic Monthly* during the 1890s, well-known physician and poet Oliver Wendell Holmes Sr. wrote, "Take a music bath once or twice a week for a few seasons, and you will find that it is to the soul what the water bath is to the body." But scientific research has shown that music is good not only for the soul—it is also good for the brain.

Studies have proven that active music making has a direct connection to how well the brain functions. In fact, there is evidence to indicate that the brain seems to operate according to patterns that closely resemble musical notes. A research team headed by psychologist Dr. Frances Rauscher of the University of Wisconsin conducted a study that confirmed a link between music and intelligence, and suggested that learning skills can be improved by listening to music at an early age.

In a section of its website entitled "Music Making and the Brain," the American Music Conference states that, "Studies have linked active music making with better language and math ability, improved school grades, better-adjusted social behavior, and improvements in 'spatial-temporal reasoning,' which is the foundation of engineering and science." Other studies connecting music to intelligence have found that music improves reading ability, reasoning skills, language skills, and can even result in improved scholastic aptitude test (SAT) scores among students.

elor's degree in a music-related field such as music history or music theory, and most music librarians have at least one year of graduate study in music, with many holding master's degrees.

Private instructors are not necessarily required to have college degrees; however, they must prove themselves to be proficient in instrumental music or voice, and have enough experience and training so that they have the talent and skills necessary to teach. If they work at a music studio or music store, they must audition before they are hired as an instructor. If they work on their own, they usually build their business through word-of-mouth referrals, which are based on how talented and competent they are at teaching.

College students planning to teach at elementary or secondary schools, colleges, or universities are assigned student-teaching jobs during their last year of undergraduate studies. This is usually the first opportunity they have to apply what they have learned in college to the real world, and as they teach, they are supervised by on-staff educators who act as their mentors and coaches.

Earnings and Opportunities

Once students finish their education and student-teaching assignments and are ready to enter the job market, the amount of money they earn is based on several things: which area of music education they have chosen, their level of education and experience, and the geographic location. Elementary and secondary music teachers' salaries range from $19,000 to $70,000 per year, with college and university music professors earning from $18,000 to $150,000 per year. Music librarians' salaries tend to range from $18,000 to $45,000 annually, and private instructors charge anywhere from $10 to $100 per hour.

In general, the largest number of full-time teaching positions exists in elementary and secondary schools. However, with decreases in funding for arts and music programs, music teaching jobs are generally more prevalent in upper-level grades, where there are more full-time music teacher positions. For music professors in colleges and universities, the U.S. Department of Labor predicts that the job outlook for college instructors will be brighter than it has been in the past. Because of projected growth in college and university enrollment, employment is expected to grow faster than average in the coming years, which is likely to mean increased opportunities for music professors and music librarians.

Once someone becomes a music educator there are many opportunities for career advancement, which are usually achieved through higher education and experience. Those who teach in elementary or secondary schools may continue working on their masters or Ph.D. degrees; once they have advanced their education, they may apply for higher-level teaching jobs, either at their current place of employment or at colleges and universities.

Music educators help inspire children to learn more about their instrument, music, and music history.

People who choose music education as a career do not choose it because they hope to become rich. In fact, music educators are paid relatively low salaries when considering the education and musical talent this profession requires. It is something else that drives these people: their love of music, and their desire to pass that on to others. The National Association for Music Education has these words for aspiring music educators:

49

The music teaching profession has a long and noble history. To associate yourself with that history—with an unbroken chain of some of the world's greatest musical intellects, music-makers, and music teachers—is personally and professionally exciting. . . . In choosing this profession you add one more link to the chain, binding yourself to others who have dedicated themselves to bringing joy and beauty to the lives of those they encounter. But, more than this, you will add an extra dimension of humanness to yourself and others by sharing the power of sound through the teaching of music. [32]

Chapter 4

Music Publicists

When a new rock band releases a best-selling CD and the members' names and photographs are splashed all over newspapers everywhere, that did not happen by accident—it was the work of a music publicist. When a popular singer is interviewed for a major story in *Rolling Stone* magazine, or appears on national television to promote an upcoming tour, that was also the work of a music publicist. These are examples of publicity, which is the media exposure given to a particular performer or group. And music publicists are the people responsible for generating it.

Publicity is a powerful thing. When done right, it can create the kind of media buzz that takes unknown performers and skyrockets them to stardom. But why is publicity so important? Because professional musicians put immense amounts of time, talent, and energy into creating their records. They write the music, play and sing it, rehearse it, fine-tune it, and then record it at a studio. It could be the best work they have ever done—destined to be a platinum-seller or a Grammy Award winner. However, the only way this music can sell is if the public is aware of it. And the only way the public becomes aware of it is through publicity.

Music publicists represent a variety of clients. These clients could be anyone from a brand-new, unknown rock band to a well-established jazz quartet, a famous opera singer to a classical guitarist—and nearly everyone in between. Some publicists work for large recording companies (record labels) like RCA, Warner Brothers, or Capitol, which employ their own publicity staffs. Others may work for publicity firms, or work on an independent, or freelance, basis.

Capitol Records, in Los Angeles, California, is home to some of the most successful publicists in the music industry.

Regardless of where they work, all publicists' jobs involve regular contact with the media, including newspapers, magazines, and television and radio stations. This regular contact is important because the more times people hear about a musician or band, see their photographs, and read about them, the more likely they are to remember them, buy their music, and attend their concerts. This means music publicists face a never-ending challenge: keeping the media interested in their clients.

No Two Days Are the Same

Obviously, with all the time they spend talking with the media, music publicists spend a great deal of time on the telephone. But there is much more to their jobs than that. They also spend time meeting with media people in person, and meet regularly with clients and members of their clients' staff, such as managers, booking agents, and other publicists. They accompany clients to media interviews and special appearances, either locally or wherever they are on tour. They write press releases and performer bios

Publicity vs. Advertising

Many people confuse the term publicity with advertising. And although it is true that the two often work hand in hand, they are actually quite different. Advertising is a paid form of media exposure, which means its placement is guaranteed. For example, if an advertisement appears in the *Los Angeles Times* about an upcoming concert, the promoters of that concert pay for the ad and they are guaranteed that it will appear in the newspaper on a given date. Conversely, publicity is not a paid form of media exposure. If an entertainment reporter for the newspaper chooses to write an article about the concert, that is considered publicity. And the key word is chooses, because unlike advertising, publicity is never guaranteed. In fact, many article ideas—called "pitches"—that are sent to newspaper editors, magazine editors, television and radio stations are rejected. This can happen for several reasons: Perhaps the concert features a musical act that is not important enough or famous enough to report on, or maybe the newspaper or news program is already filled up with other news that has been deemed a higher priority.

Advertising definitely has its place in helping to create awareness, but publicity has several advantages over advertising. For one thing, people know that newspapers and other media are not paid for the stories they run, so the perception is that they are more credible, more unbiased, and more believable than advertisements and commercials. Another factor is that depending on the media used, advertising can cost thousands or even millions of dollars, while publicity is much less expensive—the only cost is the fee charged by the publicist.

Publicity takes more work than advertising because it involves constantly coming up with fresh ideas and then trying to convince the media that the ideas are newsworthy, or worth writing about. However, good publicists know and understand that publicity is well worth the effort because of the positive results it can produce.

(background stories), and closely monitor any media coverage or articles written about their clients. Also, music publicists often attend social functions such as luncheons, parties, and events, where they can mingle with media people and get to know them.

One of a music publicist's most important functions is to constantly be on the lookout for opportunities to get media coverage for clients, and this takes careful planning. Sometimes it involves calling a newspaper or magazine editor to discuss something newsworthy that the publicist thinks might make a good story. In other cases, such as an upcoming concert tour or the release of a new CD, the publicist will develop a detailed plan for exactly how the event will be promoted. This plan will likely include promotional activities and a specific timeline for each event, a list of which media representatives should be targeted and where they are located, and any personal appearances or interviews that need to be scheduled. Once the plan is complete and has been approved by the client, the publicist prepares media kits (sometimes called press kits), which are packets of information that include a press release about the event, the performer's bio, a photograph, copy of a CD, and clippings of any major press coverage about the performer. The media kits are then mailed or delivered to the targeted media contacts, and about a week later the publicist follows up with a telephone call. This follow-up is crucial because it may be the publicist's only chance to line up stories, interviews, and personal appearances for clients.

The Importance of Relationship-Building

Savvy music publicists know that to get stories written about their clients, or to get any media attention at all, they must do more than send out media kits and make telephone calls—they must put effort into building relationships with their media contacts. In fact, they spend so much time developing these relationships that this function of their job is commonly referred to as media relations.

Some primary media contacts include entertainment editors at newspapers and magazines, television producers and reporters, and radio promotion directors, and publicists go out of their way to get to know these people. According to former music publicist Nicole Blackman, media people respect and pay attention to publicists who make an effort to form relationships with them. As she explains:

The musical group, the Spice Girls. Groups can sometimes become overnight successes with the help of a music publicist.

Sometimes I'll call an editor, not to pitch anything, but just to say, "Hi. How was your weekend? Heard you got married. What did you have for lunch today?" That stuff can really cement a friendship. Also I won't send every record to every editor. I'm not going to waste their time. Then when I'm really hot on an act, I can call him and say, "Hey—I've got something special that's really right for you." And he knows I'm serious. Those relationships mean a lot.[33]

Knowing better than to waste the media's time is a key element in earning credibility with them. As music publicists get to know their media contacts, they learn what these people care about, what their audience cares about, and the kinds of things that interest them. Publicists need to develop an acute awareness of what audience their clients' music appeals to, or could appeal to, which is identifying their musical niche. This helps them to determine what sets their clients' music apart from the music of thousands of other performers so that they can make smart decisions when contacting the media.

Record Promoters

Like a music publicist, a record promoter's job is to increase public awareness of a performer's music. However, there is one key difference between the two jobs. While publicists focus on developing relationships with the media, record promoters form those same types of relationships with program directors and music directors at radio stations. A record promoter's job is to convince radio stations across the country to play the music—and this is important because the more often people hear an artist's music on the radio, the more likely they are to buy it. A big radio hit can make the difference between a record selling a few hundred copies and being number one on the charts.

Since radio stations are bombarded with new music every day, they pick and choose what they will play on the air. Thus, before record promoters approach these stations, they must develop a keen understanding of the station's listeners and what style of music appeals to them. Then they develop a plan for persuading the targeted stations to play their performer's records. They gather band information and publicity, as well as sales figures proving how successful their record has been within certain regions or among certain groups of listeners. They may also meet with record store representatives or other record promoters to discuss buying trends, which helps them to convince radio stations that since the record has been a hit in one area, it will be a hit in their areas as well. Once promoters have gathered all their information, they visit the radio stations and make their sales pitch.

In the book *Careers for Music Lovers and Other Tuneful Types*, promotion director Ed Nuhfer says getting a performer's music played on radio is key to their success: "When you're able to secure airplay you know that you at least have a chance to expose your artist to the consumers, and if the consumers happen to like what they're hearing, they take some money out of their wallets and go to the record store and buy that record."

Just as good media relationships are important, so are good relationships with clients. Publicists must get to know their clients inside and out—their good points and their bad points, their strengths and their weaknesses. This is crucial because publicists are the link between the performers, the media, and the public. If a television station wants to interview a band for an upcoming program, it is the publicist who sets it up and attends with the band. If *Spin* magazine wants to do a feature story on a popular performer, the publicist arranges and attends the interview session with the performer. If an entertainment writer at a newspaper hears a rumor that a band is breaking up or getting a new lead singer, it is the publicist who confirms or denies the rumor. In other words, publicists are the public voice of the performers whom they represent.

Good Days and Bad Days

With all the places they go, the people they see, and the things they do, a music publicist's job could never be described as boring—far from it, in fact. That means publicists constantly deal with schedules that are often unpredictable, always hectic, and packed from morning until night with a constant whirlwind of activities. This fast pace can be exhilarating at times; however, the immense amount of details and constant juggling of priorities can also be challenging and stressful.

Music publicists represent multiple clients—everyone from young, unknown singers to world-famous bands. And just as all clients are different from each other, all clients' needs and priorities are different as well. If a publicist is responsible for representing ten clients and all ten clients have promotional activities going on at the same time, this can create a never-ending barrage of media phone calls and meetings, performer interviews, personal appearances, client meetings, and social engagements. Plus, music publicists often tour with their clients, which means frequent travel away from home. That can be exciting, but it also means publicists rarely have routine work schedules. In fact, music publicists typically work long hours, with days that often stretch into the night.

Music publicists work very hard at trying to gain publicity for their clients. When they are successful, and their clients become more successful—or even famous—as a result, this is one of a publicist's greatest triumphs. Ariel Hyatt shares her thoughts about the rewards of owning a successful publicity firm:

Red Rocks Amphitheatre in Colorado. One of the highpoints of a music publicist's job can be to watch their clients perform in large venues such as this one.

There have been so many it is hard to say. There are the obvious ones—like when my bands play Red Rocks and I stand on stage in utter disbelief at what 9,500 people in that beautiful venue look like. Then there are the more subtle ones like when I call a writer and they know who we are and they pay us a compliment or promise us they will listen to our CD and then follow through on that promise.[34]

Of course, a music publicist's job is not always one of triumphs; there can be low points as well. Dealing with the media can often be frustrating since they are busy people and do not have time to pay attention to everyone who contacts them. They can also be rude or impatient with publicists, especially those they do not know or who represent bands they are not particularly interested in. This can be intimidating, particularly to a publicist who is new or inexperienced.

Music publicists are sometimes faced with the challenge of representing clients who do embarrassing or inappropriate things, and they must make statements that will hopefully keep their clients in a favorable light with the public. This means they can find themselves in awkward positions when asked pointed questions by the media, such as "Is it true that the lead singer has entered drug rehab again?" or "How about that rumor that the band is fighting and may break up?" Publicist Heidi Ellen Robinson, who has represented stars such as Rod Stewart, Van Halen, and Jane's Addiction, as well as handling publicity for the first five Lollapalooza festivals, says in these situations the most important thing is to be honest with the media, while still protecting the client's reputation. She shares her thoughts on handling publicity challenges:

The Sting of Bad Publicity

The saying that "no publicity is bad publicity" is based on the belief that any media attention is good because it can increase a celebrity's awareness among the public. However, bad publicity is sometimes not good, and can even be detrimental to a star's reputation. One example of this is Sean "Puff Daddy" Combs, now known as P. Diddy, who found out how much damage bad publicity can do.

In the summer of 2000, after Combs had been arrested for his part in a New York nightclub shooting, negative publicity about him seemed to run rampant in the media. The editor of *Spin* magazine was quoted as saying, "It's hard to imagine anything about this is going to enhance his career," and an Associated Press reporter wrote that after a 1999 assault on a record executive, Combs had "suffered twin black eyes himself: a stiff drop-off in record sales and a sharp increase in negative publicity." That bad publicity had an effect on Combs's record sales, too: His first album sold 7 million copies, but his second sold significantly less.

With his new name, a Grammy nomination, and what seems to be a new resolve to keep his act cleaned up and his reputation untarnished, Combs may have risen above his problems of a few years ago. But he is living proof that publicity is not always good; in fact, quite the opposite can be true.

If you have an artist who commits a crime, you've got to pull the artist away from the media immediately . . . and follow the lead of the attorney. Honesty is vital here, but the future of the artist is also at stake, so the spin you put on the info you make available comes into play here, as well as making sure that media have the right facts, not just bits and pieces of rumor.[35]

The Stuff Good Publicists Are Made Of

In order to handle the many challenges they face day after day, as well as the tasks and priorities they must constantly juggle, music publicists are naturally high-energy people who like being in the center of the action. They welcome challenges, sometimes even thriving on the chaos of their jobs. And they are certainly not shy, or they could not survive in this career. Music publicists are outgoing and social and make friends easily, and they generally love being surrounded by people.

By nature, music publicists are creative "idea people," as Hyatt explains: "I believe people are either natural publicists or not. We all have friends who fit the 'publicist' description—always talking, always suggesting ideas like where to buy the best things, and always enthusiastically endorsing new movies or a restaurant they read or heard about."[36]

Music publicists deal with their clients, the media, and other professionals in the music industry on a day-to-day basis, so they are skilled at getting to know people. Qualities like sincerity, honesty, and consideration toward others are extremely important—even though it is true that not all publicists possess these qualities. In fact, some are known more for being aggressive and inconsiderate than for their interpersonal skills, and these people can give other publicists a bad name. However, the best publicists understand the importance of integrity and good manners, and they realize that how they treat others is likely the same way they will be treated.

In many professions communication skills are important—to the music publicist these skills are absolutely vital. In representing their clients, publicists talk to people all day, every day, and that means they must speak clearly and articulately, as well as being able to listen well and remember details about what they hear. In their attempts to pitch stories to the media, publicists must be persuasive enough to sell their ideas while refraining from being overly pushy. If their ideas are rejected, as they frequently are in the competitive music business, publicists cannot take the rejection personally; instead, they need the confidence, courage, and determination to keep approaching the same media people without fear—even when they feel intimidated by someone who has treated them rudely.

Sometimes publicists are successful in getting media coverage for their clients, but they may not be happy with what was written or reported. When this happens, it is essential that they keep their composure. Publicity expert Christopher Knab explains the perils of losing control in these situations:

> Watch your temper. No artist gets only glowing reviews. Bad or mediocre reviews are part of the game. Avoid the temptation to write or call back when you are emotionally heated about the story. Publicity is about making and keeping

Music publicists consult with one another. Music publicists are often outgoing people who love to interact with others.

relationships with the press. You never want to get a reputation for being a jerk or a troublemaker. If you do lose your temper, I can assure you your tirade will show up in the next issue of their publication—and no, I am not one of those people [who] believes all publicity is good publicity. [37]

Climbing the Career Ladder

Being a music publicist means having the right combination of qualities, but it also means having the right education and training. A college degree is generally required for publicists working at major record labels and large publicity companies. Although it may not be a requirement at some publicity firms, those who have a college degree—especially with a focus on public relations, communications, or journalism—usually have an edge over those who do not. In fact, job postings on websites for music publicists, or even assistant publicists, list a college degree as a necessary qualification.

Internships are extremely valuable for those seeking a publicity career, as is media or public relations experience of any kind. Blackman recommends that aspiring music publicists spend time working at a magazine, in almost any capacity, so that they gain an inside perspective on the media side of the business. And music publicist Paul Freundlich has this advice about the best way to get started:

> If you want to be in the music business, do anything you can to be a part of that business. Get in the door. If it means being an office temp, if it means being an intern, if it means getting somebody's coffee, if it means sending out the mail, do whatever you can to get into that business . . . capitalize on what you are doing. And I think with anything you do, an education can only enhance what you do. [38]

Earnings and the Future

The advice Freundlich offers to aspiring music publicists is wise because like many careers, getting that first publicity job hinges on how much work experience someone has. However, it can take time before that experience pays off monetarily.

High school or college interns gain valuable on-the-job experience, but they usually work for little or no pay. Starting salaries

Two interns (far left and right) work with music professionals to learn the music business. College students can often get internships with record companies to help them determine what area of the music industry they would like to work in.

for music publicists are often as low as $25,000 per year, with those working in larger cities earning slightly more—in general, the larger the city, the higher the wages. Experienced music publicists who have developed media relationships and have proven track records with clients can earn hundreds of thousands of dollars annually, although it takes years of hard work to get to that point.

The U.S. Department of Labor predicts that publicity-related jobs will grow significantly in the next ten years, which means the job outlook is promising for music publicists. But because of the perceived glamour of working in the music industry, the music publicity field is more competitive than most. In fact, publicity executives in major cities often receive dozens of résumés per week from aspiring music publicists. Still, the most opportunities will continue to be found in major cities like New York, Los Angeles, and Chicago.

Overall, the job of a music publicist is both exciting and challenging. It is not a career that suits everyone—but for the right person, someone who has a combination of enthusiasm, energy, creativity, and stamina, it can be tremendously rewarding. Robinson shares how she feels about her career:

> I'm not quite sure why I like this business, only that I really, really do—I love everything about it. I am so incredibly excited by a brand-new project or artist, a clean slate, a new challenge. . . . I have out-of-body experiences when someone says [yes] to me about a story, whether it's the *Denver Post* or *The Tonight Show*. I love the energy and electricity that occurs the moment the house lights go down at Madison Square Garden or the Forum and the kids in the audience know that the headliner is about to take the stage. I get so incredibly high when I have the good fortune to have connected with an artist, to know that I am in sync with who he is and what he does, and can use my ability to translate that into a successful public relations campaign.[39]

Chapter 5

Music Therapists

Music has the ability to soothe, calm, stimulate, and comfort. It can revitalize someone's mood and turn sadness into joy, and tension into relaxation. It can trigger memories and emotions, heighten the senses, and encourage uncommunicative people to talk. Music can help someone forget pain or loneliness, if only for a short time, and it can transform people who feel powerless by giving them a renewed sense of hope. In short, music is more than just pleasant to the ear—it has the power to heal. And this healing power enables music therapists to help even those patients who have been unresponsive to other types of treatment.

Dr. Oliver Sacks, a physician and author of the book *Awakenings*, shares his views on the healing power of music: "Music can be a crucially important aspect of therapy. Often people who can no longer use or understand language and cannot achieve conceptual thought can respond to music. I've seen patients who couldn't take a single step but could dance, and patients who could not utter a single syllable but could sing."[40]

No one is absolutely certain why music affects people the way it does. Psychologists, musicologists, and others have studied music's mysterious powers for many years and have developed numerous theories. Some say music has a direct effect on brain development while others say it triggers hidden creativity, which improves motivation and increases someone's desire to learn. Yet even though researchers may differ in their opinions about *why* music has such a profound effect on people, there is no doubt that it *does* have an effect on people.

Since the beginning of time, music has been used to communicate and express feelings. There is even evidence to suggest that music was used for healing purposes many centuries ago. Some people viewed it as a miracle cure. But the recognized field of music therapy is a fairly new concept that began taking shape during the 1940s, when music was used in treatment programs for World War II veterans who had suffered from physical and emotional trauma. The success that resulted from those programs prompted scientists to begin researching the potential of using music in conjunction with medicine. In 1944 the first college music therapy program was introduced, and the field of music therapy was officially born.

Music therapy is a form of treatment that combines music with emotional, physical, and psychological therapy. It is used to treat patients suffering from a variety of mental and physical conditions, such as those who are emotionally disturbed or learning disabled, as well as those who are mentally or physically handicapped. Today, music therapy has become a recognized and respected field, and there are thousands of registered music therapists practicing in the United States. In the words of Barbara Crowe, former president of

To cure battle exhaustion during World War II, servicemen were often encouraged to use music as a form of therapy.

Helping Patients Who Are Dying

When music therapists work with terminally ill patients, it is known as palliative treatment, because it is intended to lessen the patients' pain and suffering rather than to cure them. In these cases the therapist's goal is to provide comfort to a dying patient, as well as his or her family, through the use of music.

A major frustration for people who are dying is that their loved ones are in denial, and no one seems willing to listen to them talk about their impending death. But they want to talk about it, and they need to talk about it—and music therapists help them do just that. For example, a therapist might ask a patient to choose one or two songs that describe how he or she feels about dying. Maybe the song describes grief, sadness, intense pain, or memories of the past. It could describe needs and desires the patient has, or the fear of dying—or instead of fear, maybe a sense of inner peace. Music can break down barriers and allow people to freely communicate their feelings, which reduces anxiety and can replace hopelessness with contentment.

One reason music is so effective when dealing with dying patients is that it allows them to express themselves openly. Laurie Rugenstein is a music therapist working for a hospice organization in Colorado. In an article in the *Daily Camera*, she says when she plays music for her patients, it causes them to say things they may not have been able to put into words. She explains, "It's important for people to review their lives. Many of the people I work with are couples. It's a way for them to go back and remember things and events in their lives together and begin the process of letting go."

the National Association for Music Therapy, this musical approach to patient care "can make the difference between withdrawal and awareness, between isolation and interaction, between chronic pain and comfort—between demoralization and dignity."[41]

Communicating Through Music

Music therapists work with people of all ages, from young emotionally disturbed or autistic children who cannot communicate, to older adults who have lost their ability to remember the past. And the results are often quite remarkable—even people who have not responded to other methods of treatment show great improvement in their physical and psychological health.

Music therapists use music as a way to build relationships with their patients, teaching them to communicate and express themselves using music instead of words. The result is an environment that is both creative and nonthreatening, and one in which patients often thrive and dramatically improve. Music therapist Elizabeth Huss works with a variety of patients in different age groups who suffer from psychological and physical disorders. She describes the effects of music therapy on some of them:

> It's rewarding to know that you are offering something to the client, and the music is offering something to the client, that may not have been available to them before. I have clients that respond to music in ways that exceed their responses to everything else. I have a client who is severely, profoundly retarded. You could go to her room and talk to her and touch her and it will have no effect at all. But once you start playing the music she'll start smiling and shaking her head to the beat of the music. Just having that connection—bringing her out of herself—is amazing.[42]

In working with patients, the therapist's goal is not to teach them to become musicians by singing or playing musical instruments, although some patients do learn these skills during therapy. Rather, the goal is to use singing and instrumental music to create a sort of musical language between the therapist and patient. They participate together in the therapy session as they communicate with each other by singing songs; playing instruments such as drums, piano, or guitar; or just listening to music together.

Music therapists perform their therapy sessions in a variety of locations. They sometimes travel to individual patients' homes, as well as working in hospitals, children's hospitals, nursing homes, senior centers, psychiatric facilities, prisons, and schools. Music therapists are sometimes employed by these organizations or they may work for music therapy contracting companies that offer the services of their therapists on a contract basis. Others work for themselves in private practice.

Music therapy can be practiced in a class setting or on a one-on-one basis.

Music Therapy Sessions

Wherever they work, music therapists usually participate with an entire team of health-care professionals including doctors, teachers, social workers, psychologists, as well as parents or spouses. The team works together to plan a patient's individual goals for physical or psychological recovery. The music therapist then creates structured musical activities, such as singing, dancing, or playing instruments, which are specifically designed to help the patient achieve these goals.

Of course, these goals vary widely from patient to patient depending on the individual illness or disorder. For example, the goal for a child suffering from attention deficit disorder (ADD) might be as simple as learning to pay attention and follow directions. In this case the music therapist might spend entire sessions strumming a guitar while the child focuses on keeping time with a drum. Or the therapist might make up a simple song about the child's life and ask him or her to sing along while the therapist plays the piano. In either case, the therapist also uses positive reinforcement so that the child remains motivated and feels a sense of accomplishment.

How Music Affects the Human Body

The reason music therapy is so effective in treating many illnesses and disabilities is because music has a definite physical effect on the body. Studies have shown that when people are exposed to music they enjoy, it can stimulate the production of endorphins, or feel-good chemicals that are produced in the brain. When endorphins are released into the body, the result is a natural high and a decrease in the amount of pain a patient feels.

Another chemical produced in the brain, called cortisol, has almost the opposite effect on the body as endorphins. Cortisol is a stress hormone so the more of it that is present, the higher a person's stress levels. In the same way music stimulates the brain to produce endorphins, it can trigger it to produce less cortisol, which leads to decreased stress.

Music also has an effect on how fast the heart beats: The slower the music, the slower the heart rate and pulse, which results in lower stress and a sense of calmness. Of course, this means that loud rock or rap music speeds up the heart rate, which can cause a significant increase in stress and agitation, as well as energy.

Studies have shown that music stimulates different parts of the brain, including the areas that produce emotion and deep feelings. Because so many parts of the brain are involved in processing music, it is possible for musical memory to outlast other kinds of memories—which is one reason why music therapy is effective with Alzheimer's patients. Plus, music has a direct effect on brain waves, which vibrate at different speeds depending on the level of activity. Beta waves, which occur during periods of activity (or when emotions are negative) are the fastest brain waves, while alpha and theta waves are slower and occur during periods of relaxation and meditation. Peaceful music, such as new age or soft classical, can slow down and stabilize brain waves so that a person feels more relaxed and peaceful.

One of Huss's patients is an adolescent boy who suffers from mental retardation and schizophrenia. Her goal in working with him is to build his self-esteem while teaching him to control his anger and express his feelings in a positive manner. She describes how their activities support those goals:

> This particular day he had a very frustrating day in school. We started by singing the "hello" song we always sing, in which I kind of ask him how he's doing. He said that he was very upset . . . he asked for my drum . . . and he played the drum while I played the piano. He was very angry, so he was playing hard, fast, and in erratic rhythms. I supported that style, but slowly brought him away from that by playing a little more calmly and softly than he was. Gradually his drumming calmed, and became a steady, controlled rhythm. At that point he began to smile for the first time since I'd arrived. Then we talked a little bit. He said that he liked the drum, and that he had been very angry, but that he was feeling better.[43]

The treatment techniques that music therapists use on patients with physical, rather than emotional, disorders are often quite different. For example, music therapist Ryan Judd worked with a two-year-old boy who had been born with cerebral palsy. The boy's left hand was curled up tightly in a ball, he had difficulty with balance and coordination, and he was not able to jump, even onto a thin rubber floor mat. During their music therapy sessions, Judd played his guitar and sang songs about jumping, played jumping games with the boy, and then encouraged him to run his fingers over the guitar strings. As a result of his music therapy sessions, the boy learned to jump onto the mat and to open his curled-up hand to strum the guitar.

In the same way music therapy can help children like these overcome their emotional and physical disorders, it can also be effective when used with older people suffering from Alzheimer's disease or crippling pain. As with all treatment programs, therapists start by determining the patient's individual goals, and then plan specialized musical therapy sessions to help them achieve those goals. For an Alzheimer's patient, the goal may be to help rekindle memories that have been lost because of the disease. In that case, the music therapist may spend the sessions playing and singing music while encouraging

Music therapy can be very relaxing and soothing to elderly patients.

the person to recall the words to the songs. This same technique may be used with patients suffering from chronic pain; by singing along during music therapy sessions, they may be able to relax and forget about their pain, even if only for a short time.

Music therapists also work with patients suffering from severe depression, a disease that is common among older people confined to nursing homes. After leading long, independent lives they find themselves trapped in an environment where they do not want to be, which can lead to loneliness and despair. Music therapists spend time playing instruments and singing to these patients, often encouraging them to sing or play instruments themselves. Music therapist Gaile Hayes describes one of these people, and discusses the therapist's techniques of working with her:

> She sits by the window hour after hour, watching the world outside with all its sounds, colors and characters. Her posture is one of infinite sadness and despair. She clutches a white teddy bear to her breast. Occasionally her head drops to rest

The Amazing Autoharp

Music therapists use different instruments to create music with patients including guitars, drums, and pianos. One of the most popular instruments is the Autoharp, a unique instrument that originated in Germany and has been popular in the United States since the late nineteenth century. Autoharps are portable wooden instruments that have strings like a guitar, buttons for creating different chords, and a system of dampers, or a movable mechanism that rests on the strings and helps to control the sound. Autoharps can be played while held on one's lap, across the chest, or flat on a tabletop. Their sound is rich and beautiful, quite unlike that of any other instrument.

Even famous musicians such as David Crosby have been drawn to the pleasant sounds of the Autoharp.

One reason why the Autoharp is so popular with music therapists is that its music is soft and pleasant, similar to other folk-style instruments like the dulcimer and the zither. Also, while playing an Autoharp the music therapist can sit close to a patient, which creates a bond between them. And because it is relatively small and portable, music therapists can easily transport Autoharps wherever they travel to meet with patients.

Another unique feature of the Autoharp is how it can be used in music therapy with deaf children. Because its strings are more loosely strung than a guitar, the Autoharp creates more vibrations than other instruments; thus, even if children cannot hear the music, they can feel the music through the vibrations.

on its softness. A closer look reveals a shriveled and useless right hand and arm being supported by a pillow on the table of her wheelchair. . . . Someone [with] an Autoharp approaches her, touches her gently, sits down close and places the instrument between them. Fingers lightly stroke the strings; the song begins, very softly at first, coaxing a response, any response. As the moments pass, eyes meet and the music gains strength. At last two voices are heard. Eyes twinkle with pleasure. As the climax of the song nears, her good hand expresses through dramatic gesture the emotions evoked. Sadness has been put aside for these few moments. The musician has been allowed a glimpse into a life still capable of and longing for the expression of humanness.[44]

Who Is Cut Out to Be a Music Therapist?

This kind of bittersweet experience is typical for music therapists, who must be able to cope with the emotional turmoil associated with the job. This is especially true when working with people who are seriously ill or dying, and is one of the most difficult facets of being a music therapist. By building relationships with their patients, therapists get to know them personally and often learn to care deeply for them. Huss talks about the bond that is formed with patients, and shares her thoughts on the emotional effect it can have on music therapists:

A lot of what we do is care work. We build relationships with our clients. It's a very emotional thing, not just with the clients, but also because it's music, and as musicians, that's very important to us emotionally. Most of us are very emotionally involved in our work. . . . It's particularly difficult when you work with end-stage patients that are near death. You can imagine how difficult it is to build these relationships only to lose your client.[45]

Because music therapists constantly work with patients suffering from a variety of emotional, psychological, and physical impairments, they must have a strong desire to help people. That means they must be compassionate and understanding, as well as being sensitive to their patients' individual needs. And to do their jobs effectively, they need a great deal of patience. Watching someone make significant improvements can be extremely rewarding, but these improvements often happen at a slow pace. For example, someone with a brain injury may have to relearn simple tasks like speaking, smiling, or even making eye contact, and this can take a long time. Because an autistic child can have difficulty controlling outbursts or participating in even the simplest conversation, that child's progress is usually measured in baby steps. A person in the advanced stages of Alzheimer's disease may be frightened or disoriented and unable to focus on any activity, so breaking through the barriers is a long, involved process. In working with these people, music therapists must not only exhibit patience but also maintain a positive attitude, while encouraging patients to achieve whatever progress they can. And they must believe that all people have the potential to be helped in some way through music therapy, regardless of their illnesses or disabilities.

Obviously, a music therapist's whole job revolves around music, so people who choose this as a career must be both musically talented and creative. They love and appreciate many different types of music, and they usually enjoy singing as well as playing one or more instruments. Also, because their patients' treatment needs vary so much, music therapists must be creative enough to improvise their own songs, as well as plan creative musical activities and games that encourage their patients to participate.

Becoming a Music Therapist

For a person with the right combination of personal qualities, emotional stability, and talent, music therapy is a career that can be both rewarding and fulfilling. However, aspiring music therapists must be willing to commit themselves to the required education and training, which takes a number of years and can be quite intense.

Music therapists need a bachelor's degree (or higher) from a college or university music therapy program. And because all music therapists must be certified by the American Music Therapy Association (AMTA) or the National Association for Music Therapy (NAMT) before they can practice, their college programs must be approved by these organizations. There are schools throughout the country that offer music therapy degrees, and the typical curriculum includes classes in music and music therapy, as well as classes in psychology, sociology, and counseling. Also, students study human development, disabilities, and a variety of sciences, among other subjects.

With the proper training, a music therapist can learn to enhance the lives of their patients. The therapist above helps a class of students with Down Syndrome learn how to play music.

A crucial part of a music therapist's college preparation is a nine-hundred-hour internship, which is required for certification. Internships can be performed in a variety of locations such as children's hospitals, general hospitals, senior citizen centers, or other approved clinical settings and usually take from six months to a year to complete. Once college requirements and the internship are complete, students are eligible for testing to earn their certification as a board certified music therapist (MT-BC). After five years, music therapists must either retake the certification exam or prove that they have continued pursuing their professional development according to guidelines set by the AMTA.

Earnings and Future Outlook

Once someone is certified as a music therapist, he or she usually receives placement assistance from the college. Some music therapists are hired by the organizations where they worked as interns. In terms of salary, newly certified music therapists do not earn a great deal of money. Most usually start out with annual salaries in the low to mid-$20,000 range, while those who are experienced can earn up to $70,000 annually. Geographic location is a factor, since music therapists in larger cities generally earn more than those in smaller, more remote locations. Place of employment is also a factor in how much music therapists earn: Those working for large contracting companies or in private practice are able to set their own rates, so they generally earn more than therapists employed by senior centers, schools, clinics, or other nonprofit organizations that have limited budgets for staffing.

For people considering a career in music therapy, the future looks bright. Although the field is relatively new, ongoing research continues to support the value of music therapy as a treatment technique for many illnesses and disabilities. As more patients continue to benefit from music therapy, and their success stories become known, the demand for music therapists will grow—and that translates to more job opportunities.

Music therapy is not a career that will make anyone rich, nor is it a career for which everyone is suited. There are frustrations as well as triumphs, sadness as well as joy. However, those who choose this career do so because they have a strong desire to help others who desperately need help. Music therapists combine their musical talents with their abilities to counsel and teach, and in the process, they can make a positive difference in people's lives.

Although music therapists have many stories about their work, perhaps the best testimony about the power of music therapy is by a woman whose husband suffered from a severe case of dementia. She writes:

> When I was encouraged by a music therapist to sing to my husband, who had been lost in the fog of Alzheimer's disease for so many years, he looked at me and seemed to recognize me. On the last day of his life, he opened his eyes and looked into mine when I sang his favorite hymn. I'll always treasure that last moment we shared together. Music therapy gave me that memory, the gift I will never forget. [46]

Chapter 6

Recording Engineers

When a music fan takes a new compact disc out of its package, puts it into a CD player, presses "play," and cranks up the volume, that person is probably only focused on one thing: how great the music sounds blasting through the speakers. But how did all those songs get onto the CD in the first place? What happens from the time that musicians write and perform their music until a CD is released? The answer is the studio recording session. And a technical specialist known as a recording engineer plays a major role in making that session happen.

Recording engineers are creative and highly skilled professionals. They spend their time working at recording studios, inside sound-proof control rooms where they are surrounded by sophisticated technical equipment that makes recording sessions come to life. And while people become recording engineers for different reasons, they all have one thing in common—they are die-hard music fans. Well-known recording engineer Bernie Torelli shares his perspective on this: "Music. I love music. That's why I do this. Music is music, I like all kinds. I like classical, I like thrash, I like hip hop, hard rock, you know? Some people say a certain kind of music is not good. I'm not okay with that. Everybody has something to say, and they are playing a certain kind of music so you can feel what they are trying to say."[47]

Inside a Recording Session

Because of this all-consuming love of music, recording engineers take great pride in the crucial role they play during recording sessions. After all, the sessions would not be possible without recording engineers to operate the control room equipment, which includes a high-tech console known as the mixing board (also called a sound-board), as well as various recorders and other devices.

Once a recording session has been scheduled by the studio manager or producer, the engineer consults with them about what type of group will be recording, what instruments they will play, and how the studio needs to be set up. The engineer also determines how many and what types of microphones will be needed, as well as the need for any other special equipment.

The next step is to get the studio ready. The engineer sets up as much equipment as possible in the "live room," an area outside the control room where musicians play during a session. This involves placing some of the microphones on stands, running cables from the microphones into the control room, and testing them to be sure they are working properly. In larger studios the recording engineer is assisted by one or more engineering assistants or interns during all setup activities, while in smaller studios one person may handle it all.

A recording engineer adjusts a soundboard. Recording engineers operate the equipment necessary for musicians to make a record.

When the musicians arrive at the studio, the engineer helps to set up their instruments in the live room, and sets up their amplifiers and speakers in adjacent closet-sized rooms known as isolation booths. These booths surround the live room and are separated by thick, soundproof glass. The actual instrument sounds and vocals are contained within the separate booths so that they do not interfere with each other (or "bleed") during the recording session.

Once the instruments are in place, the engineer sets up microphones by each speaker and each individual drum. Then the musicians test the instruments for sound quality and volume, and the engineer makes necessary sound adjustments. When the recording

The Advantages of Multitrack Recording

When a band is in a recording session, all the musicians are positioned so that their instruments and vocals are isolated from each other. Separating the different sounds avoids what is known as bleeding, or one instrument's sound interfering with another. This is important because the engineer records the session with a device known as a multitrack recorder.

A multitrack recorder captures instrument sounds and vocals and keeps each track separate from the others. A track is simply a channel or section of a tape along which the music travels, and the process of recording in this way is often called "tracking" or "laying down tracks." Each track can be used to record a separate sound, as recording engineer Ken Lanyon explained in an interview with the author: "The beauty of multitracking is that we can record each instrument and vocal on its own track—for example, each drum has its own track, the bass guitar has its own track, and the same goes for other guitars, the lead vocals, and the back-up vocals. That allows us to make adjustments to the sounds of individual instruments as we're recording."

Recording on separate tracks also helps with the mixing process, which happens after the recording session is over. Using the mixing board, the engineer combines the different recorded tracks and adjusts them to achieve the right balance of sound.

session begins and band members start to play, they can hear each other by wearing headphones, through which the engineer transmits their music back to them from the control room.

The amount of time it takes to complete a recording session can vary. Some musicians' parts may not turn out the first time they are recorded, so they will have to be rerecorded later. Sometimes it takes days, weeks, or even months before the recording process is complete, as Atlanta recording engineer Ken Lanyon explains:

> The band starts with one song, and maybe we'll do four different takes of that song before we move on to the next one. In the first session the producer is mainly concerned with getting the drums to sound right. After that, we move on to the bass and lead gui-

Engineers must know how to manipulate all the controls on a soundboard in order to make the music sound perfect.

tars, keyboards, vocals, etc. Based on the band and how much they're willing to spend on recording sessions, this whole process can take weeks. When we recorded the Indigo Girls' latest album, it took eight weeks of solid sessions. That's not uncommon for a band as well known as they are.[48]

When all recording is finished, the engineer starts the mixing process. Mixing is extremely important because the recording engineer listens to each separate track on the tape to be certain all instruments and vocals sound good by themselves, and makes adjustments to volume and balance. The final mixing step is when the engineer blends all the tracks together to achieve the perfect sound—a creative process that can take many hours to complete.

After mixing, the engineer "masters" the music, balancing the recording so each song is the exact same volume and has the same equalization, or equal levels of bass and treble. The engineer then creates a master tape that is used to mass-produce copies of CDs, which are then packaged and prepared for distribution to buyers. Newly produced CDs may be released immediately, or the record label (recording company) may have reasons for delaying the release until a future date.

Who Makes a Good Recording Engineer

Of course all recording engineers thrive on their ability to play a major part in recording music. But the recording business is about more than music—it is about people. Engineers constantly interact with producers, engineering assistants, and other recording studio personnel, so they must have a natural ability to relate well to people. Plus, they regularly deal with musicians who care passionately about the music they have created and how it sounds when recorded. The recording engineer must understand what the musicians are trying to achieve, give them creative suggestions, and make them feel comfortable and confident that the recording will turn out exactly the way they want.

Along with people skills, recording engineers need good communication skills. This includes the ability to listen well, as Torelli explains: "The most important thing . . . to do is just *listen* and *look*. . . . I have been doing this since I was seventeen, and most of the time I just close my mouth and listen—both to ideas and to the music. And musicians respect that. If you give them their freedom, they will respond with their best music. So the ability to *listen* is very, very important."[49]

The recording business revolves around technology so engineers must understand and be comfortable using a wide array of technical equipment. They must also be interested in learning about new technology, since studios constantly update their control rooms with sophisticated digital equipment that enhances recording and mixing quality.

Two more important traits for recording engineers are creativity and an excellent ear for music. This is because the process of mixing instrumental sounds and vocals is such a creative process—and the right mixing and balancing of sounds can mean the difference between a recording that sounds good and one that sounds fantastic.

The First Recording Equipment

Considering the sophisticated technological gadgets that fill recording studios today, it is hard to imagine a time when recording equipment did not exist. However, the first recorder was only invented one hundred and twenty-five years ago. And it all came about because of the telephone.

It was Thomas Edison who invented the first phonograph in 1877. Based on his past recording experiments with the telegraph, Edison was curious about whether he could record from the telephone, so he decided to test his theory. He attached a needle to the telephone's diaphragm (the part that vibrates to generate sound waves) and as the needle pressed against rapidly moving paper, the speaking vibrations indented the paper. This motivated Edison to design a more complicated device that used the same principle. This device had a mouthpiece, two needles (one for recording and one for playback), and a tinfoil-covered metal cylinder. He gave a drawing of the design to his mechanic, who built it for him.

When the new machine was delivered to Edison, he spoke into the mouthpiece saying, "Mary had a little lamb," and the recording indented the vibrations of his voice onto the tin cylinder. To play the recorded sound back, the needle moved over the indentations in the tin and Edison was amazed to hear the exact words he had spoken. With this discovery, the first phonograph was officially born.

Thomas Edison's phonograph was the first recording device.

Although the unique device was initially a big success, the tinfoil only lasted through a few playings so buyers lost interest and sales quickly dropped. Over the next ten years Edison, as well as other inventors, worked on various ways of perfecting the phonograph using longer-lasting materials for the cylinders. And from that point on, better recording devices continued to be developed and introduced to the public.

Starting at the Bottom

Having a good ear for music comes naturally to recording engineers, because not only are they music fans but many are also musicians. In fact, people commonly choose this career because they want to work on a day-to-day basis with musicians and others who feel the same way about music as they do. They also crave the chance to play a part in the exciting process of recording songs that could someday end up in the hands of millions of fans. However, someone aspiring to be a recording engineer does not walk into a studio and start right out managing a recording session. This position requires people to pay their dues by starting at the bottom and working their way up—slowly.

Recording engineers get started in the business in a variety of ways. Many attend specialized recording schools like SAE Institute in Nashville or Full Sail in Orlando, Florida, where the average length of time to complete a program is one or two years. Still, whether they have a degree from a recording school or not, recording engineers get their real training from being immersed in studio life. Many perform one or more internships, working for little or no pay just to gain experience. Torelli explains what it takes to break into the recording industry:

> The schools are good, but . . . well, I've seen a lot of young guys go to school for recording, and when they finish, they know everything, and yet they know nothing. . . . It may be because I started this way, but I think the best way is to become an intern at some studio, and watch the musicians and watch the engineer. Ask questions: "Why are you doing that? Can you explain this to me?" Watch the sessions—*live* the sessions. . . . I get a lot of e-mails from young guys asking where they should go to school. I tell them school is good to learn the software and things, but the most important thing is to get into a studio and work on real sessions. It's just like driving a car. You can read the book a hundred times, but when you get behind the wheel for the very first time, you're just like the guy that read it once.[50]

An engineering intern may have opportunities to sit in and watch while recording sessions are in progress, or even be asked to assist with one. For a while, however, it is likely he or she will handle the mundane tasks no one else wants to do, such as vacuuming the studio, getting coffee for people, washing windows—even emptying ashtrays and unplugging toilets. These jobs are commonplace for all interns no matter how much education they have. Lanyon says even when interns get stuck with duties like picking up food orders, dusting windowsills, and cleaning up before and after a recording session, they still have opportunities to learn. He explains how this works: "The benefit is that the intern gets to watch the session happen from inside the control room when he/she isn't busy. They get to see how the engineer mics the instruments [sets up microphones], hooks up the gear, and gets his sounds up. They may even get a chance to set up some mics and other equipment."[51]

Engineering interns may perform a variety of tasks to help artists prepare for recording sessions including getting their instruments ready.

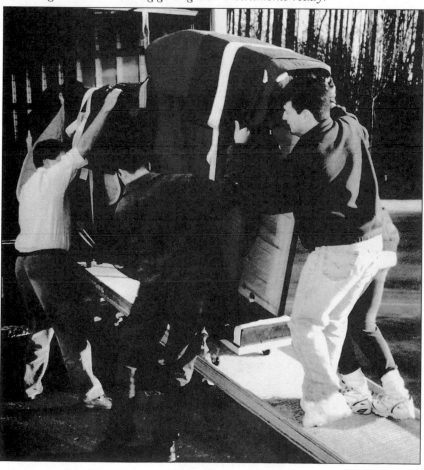

During their first days or weeks at a recording studio, interns are often in a probationary period. This is when senior-level recording engineers watch closely to gauge their attitude, motivation, and attention to detail, as well as their natural talent for the job. Those who perform their duties—even the most unpleasant duties—willingly and cheerfully, and show that they are determined to work hard and learn the business, are the ones who are apt to be offered more exciting and challenging tasks. They are also the people most likely to be offered permanent jobs.

Lanyon says one of the first indications that an engineer has faith in an intern's abilities is when he or she is given the chance to spend time observing a recording session. He explains: "This proves that the manager has faith in them and that they are doing a good job, so it would be wise for this person to pay attention. It is also important because this may be the only preparation the intern has before being placed on a session as an assistant, and you want to make sure you are ready for that."[52]

This kind of sink or swim situation is typical in a studio. If an intern has spent enough time learning about the recording process, and has shown the right kind of motivation and ability, the engineer may decide one day to let the intern assist during a session. This is the budding engineer's chance to take charge and shine, and make a positive impression on the engineer and studio management.

Pros and Cons of Being a Recording Engineer

For someone who finally makes it through the studio ranks and becomes a full-fledged recording engineer, life can be very exciting. These people exercise their creativity almost constantly, and they are around music every single workday. Based on the prominence of their studios and where they are located, recording engineers are likely to meet famous musicians, and may even develop personal friendships with them. Plus, engineers know they play a crucial role in getting a musician's songs recorded and in the hands of the public, and this can be thrilling for anyone working in this field.

While some jobs involve doing the same boring, repetitive tasks day after day, this certainly does not describe the life of a recording engineer. Just as no two musicians are alike, no two days are alike for a recording engineer. The atmosphere in a studio is often lively and

Anatomy of a Mixing Board

At first glance, the mixing board found in a studio control room looks intimidating, with its never-ending collection of switches, knobs, and buttons. Recording engineers know that every one of these controls has its own purpose, and mastering operation of the mixing board takes skill as well as experience.

The mixing board is actually the heart of the studio's entire sound system. It has several individual channels, one for each sound source or instrument. Each channel has its own separate set of controls to adjust tones such as bass, treble, or sound-enhancing effects such as reverberation (echo sound). Each control can be adjusted to change the sound from louder to softer to crisper.

The mixing board is used during and after recording sessions to adjust and balance the sound of the music. For instance, if the lead singer's voice during recording is being drowned out by the back-up singers, it can be adjusted to become louder. If the drums are pounding too hard, they can be softened. The lead guitar sounds can be bumped up for solos and then adjusted downward again once the solos are over. And if there is too much bass guitar, it can be toned down. Using the mixing board, a recording engineer can combine all the instruments and vocals to create the perfect blend of music.

Mixing boards come in different shapes and sizes. For home use or small recording studios, they may have only four channels and one master volume control and cost as little as a few hundred dollars. However, mixing boards for the larger recording studios can cost $100,000 to $200,000 or even more, based on their size and sophistication.

a bit on the crazy side, so people who work in that environment almost always have a great time doing it.

However, there is a downside to being a recording engineer that can be summed up in two words: long hours. This is definitely not a nine-to-five job and anyone interested in becoming a recording engineer must be willing to accept long workdays. Recording sessions may be scheduled for an allotted time period, but the people working on them must keep going for as many hours as it takes to get finished, as Torelli explains: "The hours. Long, long hours. Sometimes twelve, fourteen, sixteen hours at a time. Because you can't stop a session. Suppose you are scheduled to stop a session in one hour, but the singer is on it, he's inside it, *singing*. . . . You can't stop that. You have to catch it! So you go on. You stay late to get the good stuff. And then the editing, mixing, everything."[53] Even when things go according to schedule, recording engineers typically work twelve-hour shifts. Based on when sessions are scheduled, this could mean working either days or nights.

With the long workdays and the responsibilities involved with being a recording engineer, the job can be extremely stressful. The success or failure of a CD may depend on how good the music sounds when it is recorded, which means there is tremendous pressure on the studio to make the music sound perfect—much of which rests on the shoulders of recording engineers. Veteran recording engineer David Mellor describes this pressure:

> You will be in the studio day in, day out, month in, month out. Your skin will turn a deathly shade of grey and you will look like you have spent six months holidaying in a morgue. And even if you are good at your work, and successful, you will be under tremendous pressure. Artists and record companies trade on the success of their projects, and the failure of a career or a record label could just be the next single away. Inevitably you will end up taking on much of this strain yourself.[54]

Opportunities for Advancement

Even the stress and grueling schedules are not enough to scare some people away from becoming recording engineers. For them, the allure of being surrounded by music and musicians every day is reason enough to pursue this career.

Once someone has worked as an intern and is fortunate enough to be hired by a studio, he or she usually becomes an assistant recording engineer. As beginners become more experienced and knowledgeable about the recording process, they may be promoted to recording engineer positions. Mellor says once engineers become well-known in the industry, things start happening to let them know they have "made it," as he explains: "Assistant engineers seem to metamorphose gradually into engineers, but there is one defining moment when you really can say that you are a fully fledged recording engineer, and that is when you get a phone call and the manager of an established act says, 'I've heard your work and I'd like you to engineer my act's next single.' Just say yes." [55]

Earnings and the Future

Recording engineers' salaries fluctuate based on factors such as how much knowledge and experience they have, how talented they are, the type of studio in which they work, and their geographic location. Interns, of course, often work for no pay but their reward is the invaluable experience that can help them land their first job. Assistant engineers employed by recording studios usually make annual salaries starting around $20,000; those who advance to engineer status can make up to $60,000, or much more in large cities where major studios are located. Well-known freelance engineers with years of proven experience charge day rates that range from $750 to over $1,500 per day.

A career as a recording engineer can lead to working with famous artists on their next big record. The members of Foreigner, a band popular in the 1980s, participate in the mixing of their record.

As with any career that is connected with the music industry, people interested in recording engineer positions can expect to face tough competition. And while hands-on experience is often considered more valuable in this career than formal schooling, one benefit recording schools provide is placement help for their students. When seeking their first internship or entry-level job, aspiring recording engineers are likely to have the best luck with studios in smaller towns, rather than major metropolitan cities.

Overall, recording engineers love what they do for a living. They spend every day around music and they enjoy the thrill of playing a major part in the recording process. Mellor explains why, in spite of the challenges, they keep doing what they do: "Despite the long hours, the stress, and the many and varied other drawbacks to a career as a recording engineer, the excitement of capturing a musical performance to perfection is more than adequate compensation, and seeing a CD with your name on it in your . . . record store for the first time is a real thrill."[56]

Notes

Introduction: Music for Life

1. Paul Harvey, "On Music Education in Our Public Schools," *Music Is (and the Value of Music in Education)*. http://elwood. pionet.net.
2. Quoted in "Testimonies to Music," *Music Is*. http://elwood.pionet.net.

Chapter One: Composers

3. Curtis S.D. Macdonald, interview with author on February 13, 2002.
4. Macdonald, interview with author.
5. Tommy Tallarico, interview with author, March 20, 2002.
6. Scott Nesbit, interview with author, March 13, 2002.
7. Quoted in Debbie Seagle, "Nickelback: Business Savvy." www.rockn world.com.
8. Tallarico, interview with author.
9. Quoted in LucasFilm, *Stars Wars: Episode I The Phantom Menace*, May 6, 1999. http://starwars.talkcity.com.
10. Macdonald, interview with author.
11. Quoted in Andrew Druckenbrod, "Composer for 'Star Wars,' 'Jaws' and 'E.T.' Finds Inspiration Conducting on the Road," *Pittsburgh Post-Gazette*, March 29, 2001. www.post-gazette.com.
12. Tallarico, interview with author.
13. Macdonald, interview with author.
14. Quoted in Serena Yang, "Keeping Score with John Williams," February 7, 2000. www.cnn.com.

Chapter Two: Musicians

15. Quoted in Johnny Riggs, "WHFS Dave Matthews Interview from AOL." www.geocities.com.
16. Quoted in Jodi Summers, *Making and Marketing Music: The Musician's Guide to Financing, Distributing and Promoting Albums*, New York: All-worth Press, 1999, p. 44.
17. Quoted in Summers, *Making and Marketing Music*, p. 44.
18. Jacey Bedford, interview with author, February 7, 2002.

19. Quoted in Alex Teitz, "Ariel Hyatt: Making a Name for Yourself and for Every Artist." www.arielpublicity.com.

20. Quoted in Beth Nissen, "Flutist Mindy Kaufman: 'Music is a Language,'" February 23, 2001. www.cnn.com.

21. Bedford, interview with author.

22. Quoted in David Hinckley, "Vedder's Not Finished," *New York Daily News Online*, August 10, 1999. www.nydailynews.com.

23. Bedford, interview with author.

24. Quoted in Barnes & Noble, "Devil's Food for Thought," July 24, 2001. http://music.barnesandnoble.com.

25. Quoted in Nissen, "Flutist Mindy Kaufman."

26. Quoted in Jake Sibley, "Interview: Russ Miller," *Musicians' Exchange*. http://musicians.about.com.

27. *Princeton Review*, "Career Profile: Musician." www.review.com.

28. Quoted in Sibley, "Interview: Russ Miller."

Chapter Three: Music Educators

29. Quoted in *Music Education Resources*. http://musiceducator.org.

30. Nancy B. Barcus, "A Gift So Free: The Healing Arts for Our Nation's Children," *Second Opinion*, vol. 18, no. 4, April 1993, p. 42.

31. Robert Battey, "Teaching." www.cello.org.

32. National Association for Music Education, "Why Teach?" www.menc.org.

Chapter Four: Music Publicists

33. Quoted in Derek Sivers, "Nicole Blackman Interview." www.hit me.net.

34. Quoted in Teitz, "Ariel Hyatt."

35. Heidi Ellen Robinson, interview with author, March 30, 2002.

36. Quoted in Teitz, "Ariel Hyatt."

37. Christopher Knab, "Tips for Working with the Music Press," *Guitar Nine Records*. www.guitar9.com.

38. "Paul Freundlich: Publicist." www.musician.com.

39. Robinson, interview with author.

Chapter Five: Music Therapists

40. Oliver Sacks, M.D., e-mail communication with author, March 27, 2002.

41. "Quotes About Music Therapy," American Music Therapy Association. www.musictherapy.org.

42. Quoted in Jake Sibley, "Career Focus: Music Therapist," *Musicians' Exchange*. http://musicians.about.com.

43. Quoted in Sibley, "Career Focus: Music Therapist."

44. Gaile Hayes, "Music and Myth: Drawing on the Past to Enhance the Present," *Nursing Homes and Senior Citizen Care*, November 1989, p. 29.

45. Quoted in Sibley, "Career Focus: Music Therapist."

46. Quoted in "Music Therapy and the Music Products Industry," American Music Therapy Association. www.musictherapy.org.

Chapter Six: Recording Engineers

47. Quoted in Jake Sibley, "Career Focus: Recording Engineer," *Musicians' Exchange*. http://musicians.about.com.

48. Ken Lanyon, interview with author, March 30, 2002.

49. Quoted in Sibley, "Career Focus: Recording Engineer."

50. Quoted in Sibley, "Career Focus: Recording Engineer."

51. Lanyon, interview with author.

52. Lanyon, interview with author.

53. Quoted in Sibley, "Career Focus: Recording Engineer."

54. David Mellor, "How to Become a Recording Engineer: From Tape-Op to Producer." www.recording-engineer.net.

55. Mellor, "How to Become a Recording Engineer."

56. Mellor, "How to Become a Recording Engineer."

Organizations to Contact

American Composers Forum
332 Minnesota St., Suite East 145
St. Paul, MN 55101-1300
(651) 228-1407
www.composersforum.org

This organization supports the artistic growth of composers and seeks to help develop new markets for their music. It provides composers with valuable resources for professional and artistic development, and links communities together with composers and performers.

American Music Conference (AMC)
5790 Armada Dr.
Carlsbad, CA 92008
(760) 431-9124
www.amc-music.com

AMC is dedicated to promoting the importance of music, music making, and music education to the general public. The organization's goal is "to build credibility for music and music education, especially at an early age, and to expand that portion of the population that enjoys and makes its own music."

American Music Therapy Association (AMTA)
8455 Colesville Rd., Suite 1000
Silver Spring, MD 20910
(301) 589-3300
www.musictherapy.org

AMTA promotes the progressive development of therapeutic use of music in rehabilitation, special education, and community settings.

American Society of Composers, Authors, and Publishers (ASCAP)
One Lincoln Plaza
New York, NY 10023
(800) 952-7227
www.ascap.com

ASCAP is a membership association of U.S. composers, songwriters, and publishers of every kind of music. It is the only U.S. performing rights organization created and controlled by composers, songwriters, and music publishers with a board of directors erected by and from the membership.

Early Music America (EMA)
11421-1/2 Bellflower Rd.
Cleveland, OH 44106-3990
(888) 722-5288
http://earlymusic.org

EMA exists to expand awareness of, and interest in, historical music to help ensure that future generations understand, appreciate, and perform this music. Its members include amateur and professional performers, students, college and university educators, and others.

Music Educators National Conference (MENC)
1806 Robert Fulton Dr.
Reston, VA 20191
(800) 336-3768
www.menc.org

MENC's mission is to "advance music education by encouraging the study and making of music by all." Its members include music teachers, university faculty and researchers, college students preparing to be teachers, and high school honor society members, among others.

Music Library Association (MLA)
c/o A-R Editions, Inc.
8551 Research Way, Suite 180
Middleton, WI 53562
(608) 836-5825
www.musiclibraryassoc.org

MLA is a professional organization that is devoted to music librarianship and to all aspects of music materials in libraries. It provides a forum for study and action on issues that affect music libraries and their users.

MusicStaff.com
2 Executive Dr., Suite 310
Somerset, NJ 08873
(732) 868-8463
www.musicstaff.com

MusicStaff.com enables students, parents, and musicians to find music teachers, music schools, and music lessons anywhere in the United States by zip code. The site includes articles, "tips and tricks," and online music lessons.

National Association of Schools of Music (NASM)
11250 Roger Bacon Dr., Suite 21
Reston, VA 20190
(703) 437-0700
www.arts-accredit.org

NASM is an organization of schools, colleges, and universities that offer music studies. It helps guide its member schools in development of curriculum content so that students are properly prepared for their music careers.

Opera America
1156 15th St. NW, Suite 810
Washington, DC 20005
(202) 293-4466
www.operaam.org

This organization's mission is "to promote opera as exciting and accessible to individuals from all walks of life." Its membership includes singers, educators, businesses, and most anyone else who is interested in the field of opera.

Public Relations Society of America (PRSA)
33 Irving Pl.
New York, NY 10003-2376
(231) 460-1490
www.prsa.org

PRSA is the world's largest organization for public relations professionals. Its primary objectives are to advance the standards of the public relations profession and to provide members with professional development opportunities through continuing education programs, information exchange forums, and research projects.

Society of Broadcast Engineers
9247 North Meridian St., Suite 305
Indianapolis, IN 46260
(317) 846-9000
www.sbe.org

This is a nonprofit organization that serves the interests of broadcast engineers. It is the only society devoted to the advancement of all levels of broadcast engineering.

Women in Music National Network
31121 Mission Blvd., Suite 300
Hayward, CA 94544
(510) 232-3897
www.womeninmusic.com

This organization's goal is to help encourage and support the activities of women in all areas of music through education and networking services.

Young Concert Artists, Inc. (YCA)
250 W. 57th St., Suite 1222
New York, NY 10107
(212) 307-6655
www.yca.org

YCA is a professional organization that was founded to discover and help launch the careers of young, talented musicians from all over the world.

For Further Reading

Michael Fink, *Inside the Music Industry*. New York: Schirmer, 1996. An informative and comprehensive introduction to the music industry. Discusses the history of the record business, history of radio, music trends, legalities in the music business, the lives of performers, music criticism, and media, among other topics.

Susan Hanser, *The New Music Therapist's Handbook*. Boston: Berklee Press, 2000. Provides valuable information for music therapy professionals as well as students. Includes an introduction to the field of music therapy, new techniques and treatment programs, case studies, and guidelines for beginning music therapists.

David Miles Huber, *Modern Recording Techniques*. Boston: Focal Press, 2001. An updated version of the book that has been popular among musicians, students, and audio engineers for over ten years. An excellent guide, comprehensive manual, and reference tool for those wanting to learn professional recording.

Jeff Johnson, *Careers for Music Lovers and Other Tuneful Types*. Lincolnwood (Chicago): VGM Career Horizons, 1997. A helpful book for people who are interested in a music career. Explores a number of music careers and includes interviews with music professionals.

Barbara Lee, *Working in Music*. Minneapolis: Lerner, 1996. Explores twelve music-related careers including composer, jazz drummer, recording engineer, classical pianist, and others. Each chapter profiles a professional working in that particular career.

Howard Massey, *Behind the Glass: Top Record Producers Tell How They Craft the Hits*. San Francisco: Miller Freeman, 2000. Includes interviews with producers in the recording industry and an overview of the creative and technical processes in sound recording.

Lenn Millbower, *Training with a Beat: The Teaching Power of Music*. Sterling, VA: Stylus, 2000. A how-to guide for aspiring music educators. Discusses why music is critical to learning, explains various concepts and terms, and includes examples of music education in practice.

Diane Lindsey Reeves, *Career Ideas for Kids Who Like Music and Dance*. New York: Checkmark, 2001. An enlightening and entertaining book designed for young people interested in music careers. Provides information on fifteen music professions, and includes good solid advice for pursuing these careers.

Craig Rosen, *The Billboard Book of Number One Albums: The Inside Story Behind Pop Music's Blockbuster Records*. New York: Billboard, 1996. A close-up look at the creative process behind some of the top-selling albums in history. Includes stories about music created by the Beatles, the Rolling Stones, and Bruce Springsteen, among others.

Works Consulted

Books

Michael Levine, *Guerrilla P.R.* New York: HarperCollins, 1993. An excellent resource that provides a grassroots approach to public relations.

Jodi Summers, *Making and Marketing Music: The Musician's Guide to Financing, Distributing and Promoting Albums*. New York: Allworth Press, 1999. An excellent resource for anyone who wants firsthand information about the joys—and the challenges—associated with careers in the music business. Includes interviews with members of bands such as Metallica and Fuel.

Periodicals

Nancy B. Barcus, "A Gift So Free: The Healing Arts for Our Nation's Children," *Second Opinion*, vol. 18, no. 4, April 1993.

Gaile Hayes, "Music and Myth: Drawing on the Past to Enhance the Present," *Nursing Homes and Senior Citizen Care*, November 1989.

Janalea Hoffman, "Tuning In to the Power of Music," *RN*, June 1997.

Internet Resources

Diane Ambache, "Women Composers," *Ambache*. www.ambache.co.uk. Well-known British composer and pianist Diane Ambache provides an in-depth look at female composers throughout history.

American Music Conference, "Music Making and the Brain." www.amc-music.com. Includes extensive research that shows how active music making actually contributes to improved intelligence.

American Music Therapy Association, "Music Therapy and the Music Products Industry." www.musictherapy.org. A fact sheet that includes general information about the field of music therapy.

———, "Quotes About Music Therapy." www.musictherapy.org. A collection of favorable quotes about music therapy from a variety of professionals.

Barnes & Noble, "Devil's Food for Thought," July 24, 2001. http://music.barnesandnoble.com. An interview with John McCrea, lead singer of the rock group Cake.

Robert Battey, "Teaching." www.cello.org. An article on teaching music by a well-known cellist and music educator.

Ludwig van Beethoven, "The Heiligenstädter Testament," *The Classical Music Pages Quarterly*. http://w3.rz-berlin.mpg.de/cmp. The complete document written by Beethoven to his brothers after he discovered his devastating hearing loss.

Mary Bellis, "The Inventions of Thomas Edison." www.inventors. about.com. A historical depiction of the first recording device, the phonograph, by Thomas Edison. This article also includes information about Edison's other notable inventions.

Andrew Druckenbrod, "Composer for 'Star Wars,' 'Jaws' and 'E.T.' Finds Inspiration Conducting on the Road," *Pittsburgh Post-Gazette*. March 29, 2001, www.post-gazette.com. An interview with famed composer John Williams.

Donald S. Griffin, "Welcome to a Brave New (Musical) World." www.computer-music.com. Donald Griffin talks about the role of technology in the world of composing.

Paul Harvey, "On Music Education in Our Public Schools," *Music Is (and the Value of Music in Education)*. http://elwood.pionet.net. Paul Harvey offers his perspective on the importance of music being part of regular education.

David Hinkley, "Vedder's Not Finished," *New York Daily News Online*, August 10, 1999. www.nydailynews.com.

Oliver Wendell Holmes Sr., "Over the Teacups," The *Atlantic Monthly*. http://cdl.library.cornell.edu. An article included in a collection of Holmes' writings from the 1890s which appeared in the *Atlantic Monthly*.

Deborah Jeter, "Providing Learning Experiences in Music," *Teachers' Lounge*. www.musicstaff.com. An article by a music educator about what students should be learning in music classes.

Christopher Knab, "Tips for Working with the Music Press," *Guitar Nine Records*. www.guitar9.com. A column by publicity expert Christopher Knab, who offers tips for working with the media.

Larry McShane, "A Bad Rap? Backlash Is New Bag for Puffy," *Southcoast Today*, January 22, 2000. www.s-t.com. An article about Sean "Puffy" Combs and negative publicity as a result of his legal problems.

Debra Melani, "Soothing Notes." www.thedailycamera.com. An article about how music therapy treats patients with different types of physical or psychological problems, as well as terminal illness.

David Mellor, "How to Become a Recording Engineer: From Tape-Op to Producer." www.recording-engineer.net. Veteran recording engineer David Mellor shares his views on what it takes to be a recording engineer.

Music Education Resources. http://musiceducation.org.

Musician.com, "Paul Freundlich: Publicist." www.musician.com. An interview with music publicist Paul Freundlich.

National Association for Music Education, "Careers in Music." www.menc.org. An online brochure that includes information about a variety of music careers including music education, composing, music librarianship, and music therapy.

Beth Nissen, "Flutist Mindy Kaufman: 'Music is a Language,'" February 23, 2001. www.cnn.com. An interview with New York Philharmonic flutist Mindy Kaufman.

Peter Noel, "The 'Bad Boy Curse,'" *Village Voice*, March 23–April 3, 2001. www.villagevoice.com. An article about Sean "Puffy" Combs and negative publicity as a result of his legal problems.

Princeton Review, "Career Profile: Musician." www.review.com.

Johnny Riggs, "WHFS Dave Matthews Interview from AOL." www.geocities.com. Transcript of an online chat with Dave Matthews.

Robert Schumann, "Review of Clara's Music," *Clara '96 at ClaraSchumann.net*. www.geneva.edu. The actual transcript of composer Robert Schumann's essay about his wife's music.

Debbie Seagle, "Nickelback: Business Savvy." www.rocknworld.com. Personal interview with the rock group Nickelback.

Jake Sibley, "Career Focus: Music Therapist," *Musicians' Exchange*. http://musicians.about.com. An interview with music therapist Elizabeth Huss.

———, "Career Focus: Recording Engineer," *Musicians' Exchange*. http://musicians.about.com. An interview with recording engineer Bernie Torelli.

———, "Interview: Russ Miller," *Musicians' Exchange*. http://musicians.about.com. An interview with L.A. drummer Russ Miller.

Derek Sivers, "Nicole Blackman Interview." www.hitme.net. An interview with music publicist Nicole Blackman by musician and music marketer Derek Sivers.

Alex Teitz, "Interview with Ariel Hyatt." www.arielpublicity.com. An interview with music publicist Ariel Hyatt.

"Testimonies to Music," *Music Is.* http://elwood.pionet.net A selection of quotes from famous nonmusicians about the value of music. Includes comprehensive information about the nature of musicians' work, job outlook, and estimated salaries.

Eric Tishkoff, "Choosing and Using a Metronome," ET's Clarinet Studio. www.tishkoff.com. An interesting article on metronomes, including a brief history.

U.S. Department of Labor, "Musicians, Singers, and Related Workers," *Occupational Outlook Handbook* 2000–2001 edition. www.bls.gov. Includes information about opportunities, working conditions, salary projections, etc., for musicians.

———, "Teachers—Postsecondary," *Occupational Outlook Handbook.* www.bls.gov. Includes comprehensive employment projections for teachers and instructors.

Serena Yang, "Keeping Score with John Williams," February 7, 2000. www.cnn.com. An interview with composer John Williams.

"Why Teach?" MENC: The National Association for Music Education. www.menc.org. An inspiring article targeted at anyone interested in teaching music.

Websites

American Music Conference (www.amc-music.org). Includes a wealth of information about music, technology, and education. Also includes a link to a Gallup poll survey about America's attitude toward music education.

Grammy Awards (www.grammy.com). Includes general information about the Grammys including how the award originated and how artists and other professionals qualify to win.

The Juilliard School (www.juilliard.edu). This website for the famed Juilliard School contains historical and general information of interest to aspiring students.

Index

Picture Credits

About the Author

Peggy J. Parks holds a Bachelor of Science degree from Aquinas College in Grand Rapids, Michigan, where she graduated magna cum laude. She is a freelance writer who has written numerous titles for the Gale Group, including Lucent Books' *The News Media*, and a variety of titles for Blackbirch Press and KidHaven Press. She was also the profile writer for *Grand Rapids: The City That Works*, which is part of Towery Publications' Urban Tapestries series. Parks lives in Muskegon, Michigan, a town she says inspires her writing because of its location on the shores of Lake Michigan.